THE 7 KEY
OF SUCCESSFUL RECOVERY

THE 7 KEY PRINCIPLES OF SUCCESSFUL RECOVERY

The Basic Tools for Progress, Growth, and Happiness

Mel B. and Bill P.

Hazelden
Center City, Minnesota 55012-0176

1-800-328-0094
1-651-213-4590 (Fax)
www.hazelden.org

Certain excerpts in this publication are reprinted with permission from the follow-
ing sources: *The Slogans: Basic Tools for Successful Recovery,* by Mel B. (Center City,
Minn.: Hazelden, 1990); *Easy Does It: A Book of Daily Twelve Step Meditations*
(Bothell, Wash.: Lakeside Recovery Press, 1990); *Stepping Stones to Recovery for
Women* (Seattle: Glen Abbey Books, 1989); *Stepping Stones to Recovery for Young
People,* edited by Lisa D. (Seattle: Glen Abbey Books, 1991); *Stepping Stones to
Recovery for Men,* edited by Stephen Beal (Seattle: Glen Abbey Books, 1992);
Stepping Stones to Recovery, by Bill Pittman (Seattle: Glen Abbey Books, 1988).

Library of Congress Cataloging-in-Publication Data
B., Mel.
   The 7 key principles of successful recovery : the basic tools for progress, growth,
   and happiness / Mel B. and Bill P.
        p.   cm.
      Includes bibliographical references.
      ISBN 1-56838-344-4
      1. Twelve-step programs. 2. Self-help techniques. 3. Alcoholics Anonymous.
   4. Recovering alcoholics Life skills guides. 5. Recovering addicts Life skills
   guides. 6. Alcoholics—Rehabilitation Handbooks, manuals, etc. 7. Addicts—
   Rehabilitation Handbooks, manuals, etc.   I. P., Bill, date. II. Title.
HV5278.B33   1999
616.86'06—dc21   99-38956
                                                                     CIP

Editor's note
The excerpts from *Alcoholics Anonymous, 'Pass It On,'* and *A.A. Comes of Age* are
reprinted with permission of Alcoholics Anonymous World Services, Inc. (AAWS).
Permission to reprint these excerpts does not mean that AAWS has reviewed or
approved the contents of this publication, or that AAWS necessarily agrees with the
views expressed herein. AA is a program of recovery from alcoholism *only*—use of
these excerpts in connection with programs and activities which are patterned after
AA, but which address other problems, or in any other non-AA context, does not
imply otherwise.

03 02 01 00 99   6 5 4 3 2

Cover design by Madeline Berglund
Interior design by Nora Koch / Gravel Pit Publications
Typesetting by Nora Koch / Gravel Pit Publications

Contents

Introduction

"Practicing these principles" has been part of the AA experience almost from the time of the fellowship's beginnings. Key principles played an important role in the Oxford Group, which brought sobriety to AA's early members. The principles were then firmly and formally stated in the Twelve Steps. In the years that followed the writing of AA's basic text, *Alcoholics Anonymous,* in 1939, the Twelve Steps came to be adopted by many types of self-help societies and are no longer looked upon as the exclusive property of AA.

While there's no doubt that the Twelve Steps present AA principles, it is possible and helpful to use additional tools for a more thorough understanding of the main AA ideas. This is done with the AA slogans, which have evolved over time to become important tools in AA groups. Some of these slogans have become so popular that they can be seen on bumper stickers. Many of them also appear on signs in AA meeting rooms or pop up in talks and discussions. Sometimes an AA-related slogan such as "one day at a time" will even be dropped into a newspaper column or story that has no connection with AA.

What all this says is that AA principles are having a major influence in the world and are coming to be part of the general culture. This should be a positive development, as most of us believe that our AA ideas are basically good for people and can only improve the quality of life for anybody who wants to use them.

One problem, however, is that the slogans are sometimes not really understood and are simply repeated by rote and employed at a superficial level. A second problem is that simple slogans are a real turnoff for some educated people or for those who resent the breezy sloganization that is prevalent in American society. Such people have little confidence in anything that seems so simple, and they may even feel that the moralistic messages of the slogans seem trite and impractical.

But the very nature of these principles is that they should be stated in a simple form while still being applicable to a broad range of practical experience. In AA, the slogans carry out this simplification function effectively. One young woman even termed them "shorthand for the Twelve Steps."

Seven major slogans are usually acknowledged by people in AA and other Twelve Step programs. These seven slogans, or principles, are discussed in more detail in this book:

1. First Things First (Order)

2. Live and Let Live (The Great Law)

3. Easy Does It (Graceful Effort)

4. Let Go and Let God (Releasing)

5. One Day at a Time (Reduction)

6. Pass It On (Service)

7. Keep It Simple (Simplification)

What's convenient about the slogans is their broad application, which extends to almost any area of living. While our primary concern is recovery from our alcoholism or addiction to other drugs or other compulsive behaviors, our journey never stops there. We also have the ongoing challenge of trying to live in a world that's often confusing and disorderly. The slogans, if we choose to accept and to understand them, can help us with the difficult task of living in this confusing world.

Chapter One
First Things First
(Order)

First Things First

*Heaven is not reached by a single bound. But we build
the ladder by which we rise.*
— J. G. Holland

*The old saying "Rome was not built in a day" tells us that
every great achievement must have a single beginning and
must continue to be built with care. So it is understandable
that in recovery we need to be reminded that all good end-
ings depend on a careful, useful, and productive program of
progress.*

*Our recovery brings us the best things in life, but we
must never be greedy with them. Our appetite for the good
things is great, but it should never become so great that we
stop tasting each step of progress like we would taste each
bite of a good dinner.*

*It is exciting to lose the desire for our addictive substance,
but we must always stay alert to overconfidence.
Carelessness can tell us, "You've got it made; you're free."*

Today, I'll remember that many a relapse has been a
complete and painful surprise. "First things first" and
"easy does it" must always be my guides.

Heaven's First Law for Recovering People

"First things first" has the sound of a glib, trite saying. Thanks to AA members, the slogan appears on bumper stickers and is being well publicized in other ways. While it was a popular saying long before AA was started, it is now firmly identified with the broad Twelve Step movement, which has grown to deal with many problems besides alcoholism.

Like most slogans, this saying can be tossed off without much feeling or understanding. But it deserves more than that. It expresses the important principle of orderly progress. Order is so essential that Alexander Pope even called it "Heav'n's first law."

This means that there's a proper order for everything if we hope to get proper results. If we want a good garden, for example, we have to work the soil, plant good seeds, use fertilizer, and do a fair amount of hoeing and weeding. If we want to know a trade, we have to study and practice it first. If we want good friendships and approval, we have to make ourselves the kind of people whom others will like and respect.

The truth in these observations is plain to anybody—it's what we sometimes call common sense. Yet, it is a fact that we alcoholics and other compulsive people don't follow such common sense in the way we live our lives. We don't always like to do things in the right order, especially if the process is time-consuming and burdensome. We chafe under the discipline of tedious learning; we detest boring, repetitive work; and we sometimes resent the need to be more considerate of others' feelings. Though we want the rewards that others find as they live their lives in an orderly manner, we're not always ready to pay the price for it. Instant gratification and dreams of overnight success—both go hand in hand with alcoholism.

But if we're honest, we must admit that we've paid a heavy price for this refusal to do things in the right order. We came to regret the penalties of attempting shortcuts, as well as our plain refusal to follow the ordinary rules of living. Though we probably had many warnings that we were disorderly in our approach to life, we did not heed them. Nor could we blame others. When we finally reached a point of utter defeat, we had to know in our heart of hearts that the fault was ours, and ours alone, to bear.

Even in complete defeat, however, there can be good news. The good news is that it's never too late to begin practicing an orderly approach to life. AA gives us this orderly approach in succinct terms: (1) Get honest and admit your alcoholism to yourself and others; (2) find God; (3) clean up your life; and (4) help others. Do those things, and you will be in a position to become effective in other ways as well. In most cases, for example, a defeated alcoholic cannot rebuild a shattered business career or find a happy family life without first acquiring the tools of sobriety. Things have to come in that order, or they simply do not work.

So, in all honesty, we must first face the fact that drinking and other compulsive behaviors have been false, self-defeating attempts to obtain the kinds of feelings and success we can get only by right thinking and the right kinds of actions.

For all its folly, however, the drinking life does carry a lesson in the practice of putting first things first. Alcoholics have lots of experience in setting priorities, because we did put drinking first, thus showing how one consuming drive can overpower all the other needs in our lives. Alcoholism is a grim example of single-minded devotion to a destructive practice. As recovering people, we can enlist that same single-minded devotion to a constructive purpose: sobriety and good living. We know how to put alcohol first; we can also learn how to put sobriety first. It's understandable, however, that when approaching recovery, alcoholics and victims of other compulsive disorders might face a confusion of wants and desires. These wants, though completely reasonable on the surface, may compete for time and energy that should be devoted to recovery. For example, a person new in recovery may want a better job (or any job at all), better clothes, a decent home, and a new car. At the same time, there's a need for love and companionship. Another need is for a place in life and respect from others. It's also urgent to put behind the shame of recent years.

All of these are healthy human wants. In fact, it's wrong to tell people that such wants are materialistic and selfish, because desires of this kind grow out of feelings that have moved the human race toward progress. Yet these legitimate needs and wants can also become dangerous traps in sober living, if we get our priorities wrong. The problems come not with the basic wants and needs, but with failing to put such things in their proper place in our lives. Again, this was the basic problem when we drank—we compulsively put our drinking ahead of anything and everybody, sometimes even our family's basic security. In sobriety, we can make the same mistake in a different way by forgetting what are sometimes called "the basics" and going after things that should be secondary to our major purpose of finding and maintaining sound recovery.

The AA experience is that most necessary things will come

into our lives if we are patient and work for them. Many AA members like to say, for example, that they're now buying things for the family with money that used to go to the bar. It's common to hear an AA member say that he finally bought a new car for the first time in years or was able to make the down payment that meant the ownership of the family's first real home of their own. These material benefits can even be called the fruits of AA experience and practice. What had to come first, however, was an unconditional commitment to seek and maintain sobriety. If this commitment isn't there, the alcoholic will not only fail to keep sober but will also probably lose or fail to gain all the other things that may have seemed important. AA cofounder Bill W. often referred to the fallacy of "trying to put the cart before the horse." This is what's wrong when alcoholics try to rebuild their lives without understanding that sobriety must come first—and must be maintained at all costs. If an alcoholic does temporarily get an unexpected benefit without attaining continuing sobriety, the gain is often lost in the next binge. AA is replete with stories of people who have found new jobs and other promising opportunities while still drinking and have blown them away in a round of slips later on.

For example, a highly ambitious alcoholic will come to AA, stop drinking, and then take stock of what's happened in his or her life. Perhaps a string of debts ought to be paid. Perhaps the family is creating pressure through demands of its own. Social obligations may have been neglected or ignored completely.

To meet these demands, the alcoholic may take a second job or engage in moonlighting work of some kind. Or to get back on track with social obligations, there may be a special effort to spend time and energy on these affairs.

This may seem commendable to outside observers, but the result may be less or no time for AA meetings and attention to maintaining sobriety. What can happen is that the money earned in the second job simply provides funds for the next binge. Or the new social obligation turns out to be a way of returning to drinking.

Here's an example of the second problem. One AA member was an outstanding bowler. This had been part of his social life as well. Coming into AA, he discontinued his bowling activity and, at the same time, found new success in a well-paying job that even included the use of a new automobile. To all appearances, he had it made, and he was undoubtedly the envy of others. But after establishing a good period of sobriety in AA, he dropped meeting attendance to resume his bowling.

This was an unreasonable and unnecessary decision. In the first place, it was odd that he should have given up bowling completely to go to AA meetings. There is no reason why AA members should give up healthy recreation. There are probably thousands of AA members who bowl regularly in leagues and on weekends, often with people who drink. If AA members are on sound spiritual ground, they can do almost anything others do if they do not pick up a drink.

In our friend's case, however, AA meetings may have been seen as activities that were in conflict with his bowling schedules. Rather than working out a compromise plan that permitted him to do both, he chose to drop AA meetings and devote his spare time to bowling. In time, he also returned to drinking and was in serious difficulties when he finally came back to AA.

The basic error—and it can happen in many ways—was in putting something else ahead of things that were needed for sobriety. Perhaps he had not accepted his alcoholism for the destructive problem it is. It's also possible that he didn't believe AA members when they told him sobriety ought to be ahead of everything else. People who forget this often pay a terrible price, and this, too, is part of what AAs experience.

That's why the simple slogan "first things first" can have so much meaning as a principle for living. AA seems to say, to paraphrase a biblical saying, "Seek ye first sobriety, and all these other things shall be added to you." Persons who suffer from other addictions and compulsions have the same need to avoid completely the slippery slope that leads to trouble. Many other Twelve Step programs have been launched since the AA pioneers introduced their marvelous program. While each of these movements has created its own jargon and customs as it developed, the common bond with the parent fellowship of Alcoholics Anonymous is a stern insistence on facing the basic addiction. Here are a few examples:

- A compulsive gambler learns in Gamblers Anonymous that it's dangerous even to buy a lottery ticket.

- A sex addict learns in Sex Addicts Anonymous to shun salacious magazines.

- A compulsive overeater finds in Overeaters Anonymous that certain foods will trigger an eating binge.

In every case, the thing that has to be dealt with is the behavior that gets the addiction churning again. It may not, however, be enough to learn this lesson initially. We should also see that it must be reinforced repeatedly. "The price of freedom from any addiction is eternal vigilance." That is how an old saying might be modified for compulsive people. A person can make a good beginning by becoming committed to the goal of sobriety, but this commitment can get chipped away in the course of living. One problem is that we're surrounded by numerous people who don't have a destructive addiction; they can enjoy moderately the things that would destroy us. Their examples can lead us to become careless as recovery continues and other priorities come into our lives.

That's why it's not a bad thing to have a handy, easy-to-use tool like the slogan "first things first" when things become hectic or get out of hand. What is the first thing we should remember? Here's an example that one recovering alcoholic provided in a discussion meeting:

> As a recovering alcoholic, I consider my situation the same as a person with a heart problem. With any heart patient, nothing can be worth risking a fatal heart attack. If your heart fails, everything fails with it. It's the same for the alcoholic. Without continuous sobriety, there's no chance for life as we want and need it.

It is true, however, that we have duties and obligations that go beyond recovery from our addiction. What's remarkable is that a simple slogan such as "first things first" can be applied throughout life. Here are some examples:

An office manager:

> When I got sober, I thought most of my problems were solved. What I then discovered was that I always had

lots of anxiety and indecision when I faced large piles of work on my desk. I would feel burning sensations in my stomach and would build up so much tension that I could hardly sit in my chair. There would also be resentment toward my boss for piling on so much work.

Almost by accident, I discovered that reminding myself to set priorities would pull me out of the mess. It even had a calming effect, almost like a mantra, to repeat "first things first" in one of these situations. I would then see almost immediately what work had to be done first, and before long I would be trimming down the pile at a speed that amazed me.

A minister who sometimes counseled business executives:

I was working with two business partners who had a falling-out but were still trying to work together in their company. Each of them would come to me with his stories about the other partner and why he thought his own plan was best for the company. Each was trying to get me to back his plan.

I believe I performed an important service by refusing to back either plan. What I got them to see was that their first need was to end the fighting and to reestablish a harmonious relationship. Otherwise, it was better to dissolve the partnership and go their separate ways. They did agree to shake hands and make up, and it took no time at all to get the business back on track.

An early AA remembers a friend:

Our friend Butch worked in a railroad control tower near a main rail line. During rush hour, he sometimes faced congested automobile traffic in all directions, with express trains pounding in from east or west. When he lost control, Butch would simply stop traffic in all directions and let the trains pass. Then he would release the traffic lanes one at a time until order was restored. This application of doing first things first helped him keep his job for several years. Finally, the railroad solved the entire traffic problem electronically and gave Butch a new assignment that lasted the rest of his life.

An Orderly Approach to Problem Solving

Another member has worked out his own approach. He says:

Using first things first as a guide when any problem or crisis arises, I have an orderly method or approach that's rooted in Twelve Step principles:

- ☾ I get my thinking straight, eliminating blame-placing, resentment, and jealousy.

- ☾ I seek guidance from my Higher Power. Also, I discuss the matter with sponsors or others I respect.

- ☾ I make any necessary amends to other people.

- ☾ I take any action that seems appropriate, bearing in mind that it might also be reasonable not to take action for the time being.

What we're likely to discover, over time, is that an orderly approach based on our principles is always going to be better for us and for others. Our view of what's really important might also change as we continue to apply these principles. We may have once believed that winning and getting our own way were always important; otherwise, we were diminished and somehow made to appear as failures. But, recalling the advice of Bill W., we can learn that character-building and a spiritual way of life were always more important than any temporary victories along the way. We learn, too, that any victory reached by the wrong attitude or methods can actually become a longer-term failure.

Orderly Progress in Daily Life

Both positive and negative examples can lead to an understanding of doing first things first. We heard about one recovering alcoholic who derived great satisfaction from replacing the cap on the toothpaste tube in the morning. This simple act symbolized his effort to bring more order into his life. While one could be compulsively ritualistic about such actions, we have to concede that it's more efficient and convenient to attend to such details in proper order.

Far from being neat and orderly, a large number of compulsive people put up with disorder and clutter in their lives. One young woman with compulsive sexual problems lived in a filthy apartment, which belied the attractive appearance she presented in singles' bars. This contradiction occurred because her compulsion left no time or energy for the routine duties of life. We can start dealing with such tendencies in ourselves by deliberately taking actions that promote order:

◖ Replace the cap on the toothpaste tube.

◖ Take out the garbage on time and be sure to put the lid tightly on the container.

◖ Get the oil changed at the right time.

◖ Pay bills promptly and keep the checkbook in order.

◖ Clean out old drawers and file cabinets.

◖ Don't use new tools or appliances without first reading the directions.

We must also try to always be honest in facing day-to-day issues as they come up. We can learn to be comfortable with some problems and challenges, and we should face why we are putting off some matters until the last minute. This procrastination usually costs time, money, or effort. But when we do have the determination and make the effort to face the most urgent duty or issue, the rewards in personal satisfaction and well-being always come. "First things first" is, indeed, a simple slogan. But it can touch everything we think, say, and do.

Next Things Next

Still, the Twelve Step program would be shallow if it didn't provide for what is sometimes called a well-rounded life. Though it's never stated that way, "first things first" also suggests another subslogan that could be called "next things next." It means that needs and goals should be faced in a certain order—and we can get it right if we truly understand our program and what our responsibilities in life should be.

One AA member put it this way: His sobriety came first, his job came next, and his family came third. Far from putting his family lower on the scale of values, he was actually facing reality as he never had while drinking. "If I put my sobriety first, I can take care of my job," he explained. "If I take care of my job, I can support my family."

That makes sense. If we look at everything in life, we can find similar scales of values at work. We sometimes criticize people for their single-minded devotion to goals and efforts that we don't happen to value as they do. But they, too, are probably practicing a form of "first things first" in their own lives.

Living the Principle

In practice, however, we sometimes need judgment and guidance in living a principle such as "first things first." We can have a view of it that can create problems or conflicts in other areas.

One example is an AA member who held an important managerial position with a medium-sized retail firm. Thanks to his recovery, he was also in demand as a speaker at AA groups and service clubs and sometimes received pleas for urgent Twelve Step calls during the day.

Unlike people who worked at lower levels in his company, he could regulate his own hours. He soon began to spend a large amount of time in his AA work while neglecting some of his company responsibilities. A justification for this is that sobriety should always come first in one's life. We cannot, however, expect employers or others to subsidize such efforts. Unless we're given considerable latitude and unusual permission for such activities, we have no right to use the employer's resources for our AA work.

Another example is the AA member who spends little time with the family or in doing things for the family. If somebody questions why he or she should be spending every night at meetings, the ready excuse is, "I have to stay sober, don't I? Aren't we urged to attend lots of meetings?"

The real reason for this excessive meeting attendance might not be the need to reinforce sobriety, though that must always be a first need for any recovering alcoholic. In attending more meetings than he needed, the person may actually be seeking out meetings as a pleasant escape from the boredom and routines of family life. A meeting may also be a convenient excuse for not facing something that needs to be done around the house. In such cases, "first things first" still applies, but it should include things in order of their importance. Something that is obviously important—like maintaining sobriety—should never be used simply as an excuse for avoiding other responsibilities. This can be deceitful and dishonest. We do need meetings, perhaps as many as one each day, but we also need to live as mature adults in a world that demands responsible action. That, too, is one of the benefits of good AA living. If we truly do practice "first things first," everything should be dealt with in its own place and time in our lives.

Recovery

Recovery is the most important thing in your life, without exception. You may believe your job, or your home life, or one of many other things, comes first. But consider: If you don't stay with the program, chances are you won't have a job, a family, sanity, or even life. If you are convinced that everything in life depends on your recovery, you have a much better chance of improving your life. If you put other things first, you are only hurting your chances.

Chapter Two
Live and Let Live
(The Great Law)

AA's second slogan, "live and let live," is an idea involving common justice, according to Sir Roger L'Estrange. It expresses the Golden Rule, also found in the old Buddhist saying "Hurt not others in ways that you yourself would find hurtful." The Golden Rule is expressed in Islamic teachings in this way: "No one of you is a believer until he desires for his brother that which he desires for himself." Freedom is implied in this slogan.

To the variations on the Golden Rule from Buddhism and Islam, we can add this from the great Rabbi Hillel: "What is hateful to you, do not do to your fellow; that is the whole Law; all the rest is interpretation." Long before these statements, an Aesop fable concluded that "if we want our own lives protected, we must protect the lives of others."

The Twelve Step Route to Freedom and Justice

Look closely at such old sayings, and it's easy to see that they all express "live and let live"—a sort of Golden Rule of the Twelve Step movement. These simple words can be, to some, the key to freedom and justice. While our use of this slogan is personal, it may also be the best rule for society. What we're talking about here is attitude more than actions. Most of us have not been openly violent toward others and probably not physically abusive. But we've held thoughts and attitudes that at times can be vicious or even close to murderous. Hand in hand with such thoughts has been a contempt for certain people, either because they were too low or too high in our judgment. We have condemned them in thought and speech, in effect saying that they had no right to be themselves and to live their own lives. And bad attitudes, if held deeply, eventually translate into corresponding wrong action.

Along with bad attitudes toward others, many of us, in our drinking years, held muddled views of freedom. We thought we were strong believers in freedom. We may have even believed that we understood justice. Nothing delighted us more than to sneer at the hypocrisy and prejudices of others, especially people who were opposed to drinking. We liked to believe that we were tolerant though drunk, and fair though morally loose in many areas. If the price wasn't too high, we even acted as champions of the underdog, often because this gave us a reason to oppose people we hated and resented. In effect, this was sometimes a case of wrongly using good causes.

The Twelve Step program and groups, however, showed that most of these beliefs were shallow and selfish. The dominant idea was to get all the freedom we could possibly have to continue drinking. We demanded fair treatment for ourselves when our own behavior threatened to bring punishment down on us. When jailed for drunkenness, some of us provoked police officers and then assailed them for their brutality. Behaving badly ourselves, we reached desperately for ways to shift blame onto others.

This is not to say that there aren't great evils in society and the world. In fact, we may have received unjust treatment in the jails where we landed or in the state hospitals where many of us became patients. Through the Twelve Step program, however, we can learn the humility necessary for recovery and begin to accept that we are not equipped, in our drinking state, to deal with the world's social evils. Still, we can make a small start by straightening out our own thinking and our own lives. When we were thinking badly and acting wrongly, we were adding to the world's injustices, not correcting them. The freedom an alcoholic seeks is only a form of license to do anything. This distorted view of justice amounts to seeking absolution for ourselves and punishing those we envy and resent.

Yet, we should not be too hard on ourselves once these facts hit home. In the sickness of alcoholism and compulsion, there was bound to be distorted, twisted thinking— and perhaps we were fortunate that our behavior was not even worse than it proved to be. We could even say, given all the circumstances of our problem, that we had no choice except to think and behave as we did—that we were driven people, controlled by the thoughts and emotions of our insanity.

In the Twelve Step program, however, we can start over. We are given new choices as well as an opportunity to clear away the wreckage of the past. By taking personal inventory and heeding the experience of those who have gone before us, we can make a conscious decision to change old ways of thinking and acting and to adopt a new attitude toward ourselves and others.

It turns out to be an example of becoming adults in the

right way. In its true meaning, "live and let live" enables us to grow up and to acquire the maturity that most alcoholics and other addicts are said to lack. It requires us to become responsible people—responsible for our actions, our words, and, above all, our thoughts and feelings. At the same time, we are relieved of the "responsibility" for controlling and manipulating others.

How can members of Twelve Step groups practice "live and let live"? There are four simple ways to begin, four "don'ts":

(Don't gossip.

(Don't criticize.

(Don't try to change others.

(Don't justify any resentment.

A few comments about each of these will show how such simple practices can help build a "live and let live" outlook in our lives.

Don't Gossip

We hear lots of warnings about gossip, but this doesn't always stop the practice. As Twelve Step people, we sometimes justify gossiping about others by declaring that we're only trying to understand them. We're probably gossiping if we preface a remark this way: "I don't want to take Jim's inventory, but . . ." This is a sneaky way of masking gossip in such form that it appears to be moral and right. But for our own well-being, we must learn that any kind of gossip is destructive to peace of mind. We're only deceiving ourselves when we try to dress it up in a good motive. This is no more honest than any other subterfuge we might employ to do something wrong.

Here is how one recovering person—who is also a writer—views the way the Twelve Step program changed his views on gossip:

> I once worked in an office where some bright young men used their coffee breaks as endless gossip sessions. I was flattered to be admitted to their group, because they were well-educated and seemed to have the sophistication and confidence I wanted for myself. But I always felt uneasy after the gossip sessions were over. The uneasiness blossomed into guilt when I encountered a person whom we had maligned with our cruel gossip.
>
> Realizing that these sessions went against my Twelve Step principles, I began to withdraw from participation, first by not contributing to the gossip and then by tuning out things that I didn't want to hear.
>
> In the process, I made an astonishing discovery: The less I gossiped, the less I feared being a target of gossip! Any fear I had of being scorned and ridiculed was directly tied to my desire to scorn and ridicule others. Once rid of such desires, my entire thinking about gossip changed radically. I still like to have good things said about me. I still like approval from others. But what's more important than what others think of me, good or bad, is to live above the spite and malice that much gossip entails.
>
> I also discovered that this new attitude was important

to my work as a writer. At times, I was assigned to write critical essays and argumentative articles. The Twelve Step program enabled me to be critical and reasoning without being spiteful and nasty. The old cliché about "disagreeing without being disagreeable" became a useful guide. In this spirit, I also lost interest in reading books and articles that exposed prominent people or cut them down to size in some way.

Avoiding Gossip

Tale-bearers are as bad as the tale-makers.
—Richard Sheridan

What *we talk about, not* whom *we talk about, is one of the ways we place principles above personalities and practice our Twelfth Tradition. At meetings and over coffee, it's tempting to pass along things we hear about other people who share our recovery.*

Before we gossip or find fault with others, wise members teach us to ask ourselves three questions: "Is it true?" "Is it kind?" "Is telling it important to help someone's recovery?" If we can't say yes to each question, we mustn't repeat the gossip. If a single word from us hurts someone else, our guilt could throw us back into addiction. Our gossip could cause someone else to lose faith in the program and throw them back into addiction.

I will not gossip. Let me talk about principles, not personalities.

LIVE AND LET LIVE (The Great Law)

Don't Criticize

As recovering alcoholics, some of us found it almost impossible to accept any kind of criticism. The slightest reprimand or suggestion was like a personal attack. Even friendly or helpful criticism made some of us bristle, and sometimes we retaliated by denouncing our critics.

Despite this sensitivity, we sometimes felt that we had the right or even a duty to criticize others. When our criticism brought an angry reaction, we were baffled. After all, we had only wanted to help! We learn in the fellowship that there are good reasons why we have difficulty accepting criticism. Many of us are insecure and can easily be plunged into self-doubt. We may also resent what we see as the arrogant, superior attitude of the person who criticizes us. We suspect—perhaps rightfully at times—that the criticism is a disguised way of putting us down. We experience the wrong kind of criticism as a form of murder because it kills our confidence and self-esteem.

CRITICS CAN BECOME BENEFACTORS

We can start finding our way out of this problem by admitting that criticism has a rightful place in human relationships. There are times when we need the information that our critics can give us. We don't need to be put down, but we do need any guides to improvement that are offered in this criticism. The right sort of critic can be a far better friend than the person who tells us simply what we like to hear.

This need for useful criticism was explained many years ago by Bill W. When the AA fellowship came under attack in magazine articles, his answer was that "our critics can be our benefactors." Though criticism is hard to accept, it becomes more palatable if we try to find value in it for ourselves. Our reward for enduring such discomfort is that we might avoid future mistakes and become more effective in areas where we have fallen short. Many of us can truthfully say that we eventually found value even in criticism that was so poorly presented that at first we felt only blind rage. Later on, perceiving the truth in this painful criticism, we quietly corrected personal problems that may have been costly to us. Since some of those problems may have included bad work habits, we listened to these critics and were forced to make improvements to survive. Looking back at the experience, we had to concede that we were the people who received the most benefit in the long run.

When We Must Give Criticism

We might also be in a position where we must criticize the performance or behavior of others. We might, for example, supervise someone whose work performance is below standard. We cannot evade this responsibility by glibly mouthing "live and let live" and allowing the poor performance to continue. If we do, we are not helping the person, and we are evading our responsibilities to the organization or business.

Our slogan does give us the right approach for the difficult time when we must give needed criticism. Thinking in terms of "live and let live," we can start by eliminating any anger or contempt we might be feeling. It's a good idea to turn the matter over to our Higher Power before proceeding. It's also important to make sure that the criticism is going to be about specific behavior or performance, and not become personal.

In these situations, "live and let live" reminds us that our purpose most always be to build up and improve matters, never to destroy. Given in the right spirit, criticism can be constructive and profitable for everybody. In giving what's usually called *constructive criticism,* we should be open to the idea that we might also be at fault. One member of our group remembered a time when he was required to give helpful criticism to a sales representative whose approach had been almost ludicrous in seeking to obtain the company's business. The discussion turned out to be a good session that eventually resulted in a business relationship. In the discussion, it came out that the company's attitudes and a number of comments had contributed to the representative's insecurity. Some of his behavior was, therefore, an inept reaction to feelings that had been projected toward him. Though he was still responsible for his own actions, others were not entirely blameless for creating an uncomfortable relationship. They needed to change their attitudes.

Even when criticism does bring about a needed behavioral change in others, let's not become addicted to criticism. The line between criticism and nagging can be fine. To a certain extent, the ability to criticize also gives us a certain amount of power over others. This is the sort of thing that can easily be abused.

Judging Others

Does this sound familiar? You hear about someone's behavior or character defects from someone else. Then you observe this person (based on your opinion and assuming what you were told is true) exhibiting this kind of behavior, and of course this is proof enough for you. So naturally you cannot contain your resentment, jealousy, fear, and so on, and you feel you must share this in turn with another person instead of your sponsor.

Perhaps, if you're lucky, the things that you say will be kept in confidence by this other person; but as the saying goes, "As soon as you ask someone 'Please don't say anything,' you've given them the reason to say it."

But as most often happens, eventually the original party with this character defect will get wind of what's being said. God knows how sensitive we in recovery are! Who knows what this person will decide to do. Maybe they won't go to "that" meeting anymore. Maybe friendships will be destroyed. Maybe they will drop out of the fellowship altogether.

If your conscience starts working on you, maybe, just maybe, you may start wondering if what has been said isn't true. Maybe this person doesn't have this character defect. Maybe you'll wonder if you really know this person and understand the person's motives. You might start asking yourself: "Have I ever done the same thing myself?" "Maybe I was just assuming because of what it looked like." "Don't I have character defects too?" "Have I ever talked with this person and tried to understand?" "Do I have the right to judge what's in another person's heart, especially when I've been the brunt of another's gossip and, understanding my own motives, knew full well it wasn't true?"

As Shakespeare once said, "What's done cannot be undone." We must eventually pay the consequences for our actions. But we do have a solution, through the Twelve Steps, that can, with an honest effort and willingness on our part, set right these wrongs.

We can work a Fourth, Fifth, or Tenth Step to enable us to see what character defect of our own (anger, fear, jealousy) was responsible for our action. We can work the Sixth and Seventh Steps if we honestly don't want to keep behaving this way. We can work the Tenth Step and admit we were wrong in our action even if our opinion of this person remains the same.

Most importantly, discuss with our sponsors first how to make amends and what should be said. If we do this on our own, we may be clearing our own conscience at another's expense and so disregard the warning, "except when to do so would injure them or others."

Don't Try to Change Others

It may seem strange to move from the idea of constructive, helpful criticism to the idea that we must not try to change others. The point is that we have a right to be concerned about performance or behavior that affects us. We have no right to demand that others change or to say that others are not fundamentally acceptable as they are.

The world has never lacked for people who believe that they have a right, and even a duty, to change others. This is certainly not "live and let live," but rather a demand for power over other people's lives. We've learned through sad experience that few people can be trusted with such power. In fact, the world's painful history shows that these power-seeking people are usually persons we should never want to have as good human models. At the same time, we've also learned that few people are safe judges of what others ought to be. Much of the time, people who want to change others are trying to mold others in their own image.

It's true that most people who want to change others explain that they're only trying to make the world a better place. While this serves as a rationale for seeking power over people's lives, it also disguises another motive: the desire to avoid change for ourselves. If we can focus on the short-comings of other people, there's less time to be concerned about what's wrong in our own lives.

If we've been involved in causes devoted to changing other people, it may take some practice to switch to the idea of changing only ourselves. But it can be liberating to take on the lifetime job of self-improvement while leaving others free to be themselves. In time, it can lead to an astonishing discovery: We can be an agent of change in others, but only by setting a good example of better living in our own lives. The slogan could properly be rephrased as "Live the Twelve Step Program So Others Will Want to Live It Too."

Don't Justify Any Resentment

Resentment has been recognized as the number one prob-lem for alcoholics since AA began, and it seems to be equally destructive in people with other compulsions and addictions. One of the best ways to learn how to live and let live is to start coming to terms with whatever resentments we're aware of here and now.

It almost always seems costly to do this because of the vested interest we build up in our grudges and grievances. We justify our resentments, and often the justification is so sound that almost anybody would agree that we have a right to be angry. Most of us know any number of people, in fact, who have been the innocent victims of treachery, fraud, and tyranny. Shouldn't they be resentful?

The big problem with resentment is that it always poisons us, not the person we're learning to hate. This mental and emotional poison immediately compromises our capacity for living joyously and happily today. None of us has ever been comfortable or happy while experiencing resentment. Many times, we've become even angrier that "somebody should be causing me to feel this way." An anonymous writer explained the problem in "Resent Someone" in a publication titled *The Cocoon:*

The moment you start to resent a person, you become his slave. He controls your dreams, absorbs your digestion, robs you of your peace of mind and goodwill, and takes away the pleasure of your work. He ruins your religion and nullifies your prayers. You cannot take a vacation without his going along.

He destroys your freedom of mind and hounds you wherever you go. There is no way to escape the person you resent. He is with you when you are awake. He invades your privacy when you sleep. He is close beside you when you drive your car and when you are on the job. You can never have efficiency or happiness. He influences even the tone of your voice. He requires you to take medicine for indigestion, headaches and loss of energy. He even steals your last moment of consciousness before you go to sleep. So—if you want to be a slave—harbor your resentments!

We can get a handle on resentment simply by deciding not to permit any justification for it. An alcoholic learns, in Alcoholics Anonymous, never to justify taking a first drink. Following that same idea, it becomes possible to take the same rigorous approach to resentments.

Some people object to such an approach because it seems to be a groveling acceptance of injustice and abuse. It's the other way around: free of resentment, we can actually be much more effective in demanding and receiving fair treatment.

It Happens Over Time

All of these suggestions can be like daily exercises aimed at building a new outlook. It's not likely that merely stating "live and let live" from time to time will bring a quick change of attitude. But a persistent effort to be more understanding of others will bring a gradual change in our personality. At Twelve Step meetings, people will share their problems and feelings with us, helping to tear down the barriers that have stood between us and others. We will begin to see more clearly that we're all made of the same stuff. We all breathe the same air and have similar hopes and fears.

Conscious contact with our Higher Power will bring us to a deeper understanding of "live and let live." We're continuously reminded that God, as the author and giver of all life, cannot really prefer one person's life over another. Our life is something we received from our Higher Power and, in a sense, share with all others. As we freely acknowledge another's right to freedom and justice, we affirm the same for ourselves. It always works.

Chapter Three
Easy Does It
(Graceful Effort)

Why did an idea such as "easy does it" find its way into the Twelve Step programs?

One possible explanation: It was offered as a way of curbing the terrible excesses that seem to grip most compulsive people. Almost from the first meeting of recovering alcoholics, members have said they did all things in excess. There was a tendency to overwork, to overplay, to overstudy, to overplan—everything over and above the pace others were setting for the same activities.

With such tendencies, we should have been extraordinary achievers. It never worked that way because we often practiced our faults in the extreme too. The person who overworked also overdid his loafing periods; the person who made all his sales the first week then took the rest of the month off, and so on. We lacked the normal, rhythmic pace that human beings need to develop in their lives.

For this reason, a reminder such as "easy does it" can be an important guide for us. It helps us deal with fear, overambition, panic, stressful eagerness, and all the other pitfalls that confront compulsive individuals. At the same time, however, it conveys the idea of accomplishment—of eventually doing what we need to do.

The guiding principle that flows out of "easy does it" is graceful effort. This is a sort of effort that comes from confidence and maturity rather than the fearful striving that often results in rash actions leading to failure.

A few warnings are in order here, because *effort* is greatly misunderstood. The moment the word is mentioned, some of us begin to tense up and set our teeth on edge as if preparing for something that is going to require strain to the point of exhaustion. We gear up for battle rather than for a reasonably paced program of activity. There can often be an anxious feeling that we might not be able to achieve up to our expectations.

We do not need this sort of turmoil and doubt. Maybe we need a better understanding of what effort should be for the person who is trying to live sober. We were always told that nothing comes without effort. On the other hand, we may have heard that too much effort defeats itself. We know from experience that we often summoned superhuman effort to accomplish something and yet failed miserably, while others who seemingly made little or no effort sailed right past us. So what are we to do and how are we to apply effort between the maxims, which seem to contradict each other?

Doing Our Part, Not the Work of Two People

In Twelve Step programs, "easy does it" means starting with a confident, realistic attitude that helps shape whatever action we ought to take. Don't attempt to accomplish too much too soon. To be successful, it's wise to put aside those grand dreams of huge victories that have little relevance to our past record and current abilities and opportunities.

Rather, start with realistic goals where success is almost guaranteed if we do our part. Most likely, for example, we can do something well today even if we dislike it and wish that we could advance into better circumstances.

If we do our duty, we should accept ourselves as successful people and "winners" in AA terms. One member was temporarily upset when somebody suggested that he was not progressing rapidly enough in his work—that he should be preparing for something higher than the factory assembly-line job he held. But this view of his "progress" was only an opinion that turned out to be false when measured against his real growth, which he was able to appreciate after a little reflection.

What had he accomplished with AA's help? During his first two years of sobriety, he had changed his life in several important ways. Once a chronic absentee, he had finally learned how to get to work on time. Previously resentful and rebellious on the job, he was now meeting the expectations of his supervisor. Once completely irresponsible and dependent, he had begun to pay his bills regularly and make his own way in the world. For the first time in his life, he had held one job for more than a year. Most important, he had learned to put AA meeting attendance and AA matters first in his life. This was success, even if others outside the program may have considered him an underachiever because he was working at a job that seemed below his potential. This success had been developed slowly and easily, one day at a time.

He could have made a serious mistake by allowing the critical attitude of another to force him into an ill-advised job switch to "prove" himself before he was ready for such advancement or change. While we may have conditioned ourselves to believe that we must prove ourselves to others, there is no such need if we have accepted ourselves and follow what is given us in the program. AA members should never judge themselves or others by the opinions swirling around in our competitive and often chaotic world. We are following a different set of standards, partly because many of us came to grief in the mad pursuit of money and success. On this new basis, we should not let ourselves be pressured into actions that put us under continuous strain and fear. On the other hand, situations arise that seem hard to approach in an easy, confident manner. We could be challenged by new opportunities that seem frightening at first. We could be forced to take part in something where a successful outcome is much in doubt. Nonetheless, we'll do our best without feeling defeated or bitter. There have been numerous examples of AA members who took on responsibilities and challenges that seemed almost too much at the time. Yet, by practicing the program and maintaining confidence, they achieved surprising results.

One great secret in such accomplishment lies in the spiritual part of the Twelve Steps. It's common to hear AA members say that their Higher Power gave them the guidance and power to achieve extraordinary things. In these cases, individuals are still practicing "easy does it" but have put themselves in touch with additional power. Emmet Fox compares this to a person lifting a heavy load by operating a huge electric hoist. "The operator would not dream of trying to pull up that load with his muscles," Fox points out. "He would tire himself out, possibly damage himself seriously, and make no impression on the task in hand.

"What he does do," Fox continues, "is quite gently to

throw a small switch and leave it on. Then the electric power without any effort or fuss raises the load to any height required, and as often as may be necessary."[1]

This is a simple example, but it makes the point. In facing many of our tasks, we may be much like a person who is "trying to pull up that load with his muscles" rather than one who is letting electric power do the job. If we saw such a person straining to lift an impossible load, we would consider the person stupid rather than congratulate the person on at least trying to do something. Many jobs and challenges in the world can't be met without the addition of some greater power, and that also seems to be true of an alcoholic's life. "Without help, it is too much for us." This applies not only to staying sober, but also to the many problems and challenges of living. For that reason, "easy does it" has its highest and best application in working the Twelve Step program itself, especially in the beginning months. There are hidden problems in moving from a life of continuous failure to the conditions of sobriety. Some recovering people mistakenly set too many goals and attempt to do too much in the beginning. It is reasonable to attend meetings every day and to do anything that seems advisable to strengthen recovery. Other things, however, should be postponed or dealt with later.

One danger in early recovery is in attempting to repair damages too quickly. In becoming sober, some alcoholics also become fired with ambition. They want to pay off their debts, get a promotion that's been delayed, or make up for

---

1. Emmet Fox, *Make Your Life Worthwhile* (New York: Harper, 1946), 49.

years of waste and neglect. They might start working two jobs, which usually means cutting back on meeting attendance. In time, they're likely to eliminate meetings completely, if only to get needed rest.

This is always risky. "Easy does it" means that we do each day's work as it comes, but we do not have to do the work of two people. If we cannot meet our expenses, perhaps we should change our lifestyle or reschedule our debt payments. In any case, we must never do anything that puts a cloud over our efforts to stay sober. Recovery always must come first.

Don't Carry a Cause to the Extreme

Another hurdle for compulsive people is in becoming overly aggressive in pushing a cause or an idea. We can even become too pushy in carrying the Twelve Step message. Bill W. believed that he failed to help others during his early months of recovery because he preached to them. Though he never lost confidence in his principles, he really began to carry the message only when he toned down his preaching and simply shared his own story.

We can easily understand why a light, easygoing approach works best in dealing with others. We compulsive people tend to be touchy, sensitive, rebellious, and suspicious. When people come on too strong, we back off. We like the extended hand rather than the upraised fist or the pointed finger. If we're not careful, however, we can slip into fist-shaking or finger-pointing simply because we believe we're right. This always backfires.

EASY DOES IT (Graceful Effort)

Don't Let Excitement or Fear
Carry Us to an Extreme

Another troubled area for many of us is in managing our feelings. While we may work diligently to banish self-pity and resentment, we may overlook other dangers. Many alcoholics have great difficulty in putting up with boredom. We attempt to relieve boredom by seeking excitement of various kinds. In the right place, excitement is probably something most of us need at times. But excitement and excitement-seeking can be toxic. In the height of excitement, our reason and judgment can be seriously impaired. Unless we're fortunate, out-of-control excitement is certain to cause trouble, as in this personal account:

> Early in my sobriety, I discovered how susceptible I could be to the lure of excitement. In one case, I became involved with a persuasive person who wanted me to join him in what appeared to be a promising business venture. My reason and common sense told me that the venture wasn't all that good. As I listened to his inspirational salesmanship, however, I was temporarily swept away by the promise of overnight success.
>
> Judgment did prevail at last, and I withdrew from the agreement without any losses. The profit was in discovering how this sort of excitement seemed almost like being drunk. There was even a slight hangover when it was brought to a close.
>
> The experience also taught me to deliberately back off—to take it easy when I found myself in the grip of something exciting. I can always negotiate a better car

price, for example, if I'm not caught up in new-car fever. I can deal more objectively with other people if I haven't been overwhelmed by their personal attractiveness and charm. I can make better decisions if I think things through rather than respond to the whims and prejudices of the moment.

Along with being driven by excitement, we can also be twisted by fear of one kind or another. At these times, while fear does remind us to avoid panic and to begin working on the problem in a sensible manner, the mere repetition of "easy does it" may be of little use in destroying fear. A feeling of intense fear is usually a call for action of some kind. What helps many people is to take at least one step to deal with the problem, whatever it is. If we do something in a purposeful way, it tends to reduce panic and confusion.

It also helps to size up any problem or threat by asking ourselves, "What is the worst that can happen here?" Quite often, fear and consternation are far worse than the problem itself. This tells us that much of the problem is the fear that we have brought into it.

Turning It Over to Our Higher Power

The choice we always have is to turn any problem over to our Higher Power. We can do this successfully when we're able to believe that we are working with God on this problem. We then find ourselves moved to take certain steps that work with other things to bring about a solution.

Sometimes a lot of work on our part is required; at other times, the problem virtually solves itself. But whether our role is large or small, it always seems to be easier when we handle things in this manner.

It's reasonable to believe that things work this way because a principle of graceful effort is the way everything works in nature and in the universe. It is always possible to find easy, graceful rhythms in the natural world around us. Everything in nature has its space and its season. Fear, strain, and struggle are human inventions, and they usually bring wear and tear rather than real accomplishment. The more we become laid back and willing to accept ourselves as simply individual players in the universal system, the more successes we have in everything we do.

Surrender

I can't . . . God can . . . I think I'll let Him.
—Anonymous

We have all lived with the idea we could do anything. We have seen spaceships sent to other planets. We can send a letter over a phone line. How, then, do we come to terms with our limitations? How do we teach ourselves to say, "I can't"? Where do we learn to trust our limitations and believe that God can take us places we cannot take ourselves?

Our program tells us to stop trying to manage the world. We will never be all things to all people. Our whole trouble was the misuse of willpower. When we lower our expectations, we are not setting our sights on lower goals. We are

---

surrendering ourselves to our Higher Power. We are asking help to be better than we are.

I need to remember that *surrender* doesn't mean *give up.* It means admitting to my Higher Power that I need help to reach my goals.

When "easy does it" is quoted in Twelve Step meetings, some members add, "But do it!" This is a reminder that we can't use the slogan as a pretext for avoiding all responsibility for action. If something must be done, then we have to take steps to do it. Still, we should take these steps with confidence, maintaining a relaxed manner that helps us to control our powers of mind and body. With a truly easy and confident attitude, we will do it!

Chapter Four
Let Go and Let God
(Releasing)

"I've attended enough Twelve Step meetings to learn my ABCs," a recovering person said. "You'll find them all in the fifth chapter of the AA Big Book."

These ABCs are read at most meetings:

A. That we were alcoholic and could not manage our own lives.

B. That probably no human power could have relieved our alcoholism.

C. That God could and would if He were sought.[1]

The ABCs of Recovery

If there's one slogan that neatly sums up these ABCs, it's "let go and let God." This slogan applies not only to alcoholism and other addictions and compulsive disorders, but also to the baffling life problems that engulf all of us. We have to

---

1. *Alcoholics Anonymous,* 3d ed. (New York: AA World Services, 1976), 60.

say that we are powerless to solve any number of human problems. The answer, if it is to come, must be through our Higher Power.

This is not what most of us learn while growing up. Many of us can remember getting many lectures on the virtues of self-reliance. We were often told, "You can do anything you put your mind to." As for God's role in human affairs, we were also told that "God helps those who help themselves." Even in AA we are often reminded to "pray for potatoes, but grab a hoe!"

Given such messages, it's small wonder that many new-comers to Twelve Step programs are confused. Is God in this thing, or isn't God? If it's only grabbing the hoe that gives us potatoes, why should we pray at all? Is God limited and able to help only those who help themselves? What provision does this make for people—and this includes all of us at various times—who can be completely helpless? In looking at such riddles, we should realize that two things must always work together as we practice "let go and let God":

1. As in Step Eleven, we must have strong belief and persistence in seeking, through prayer and meditation, a conscious contact with God as we understand God.

2. Then, in the light of this understanding, we have to carry on our normal work and activities, making the changes that seem to be indicated from time to time. If our prayer and meditation have been in the right spirit, we should find guidance and assistance coming to us in surprising ways.

These two things can create new pitfalls growing out of our human shortcomings. For one thing, self-will can lead us into all sorts of delusions and traps. It's noteworthy that Bill W. warned against such problems. If we do foolish and harmful things, it's no justification to say that "God led me in that direction." Most likely, we were only following our own wishes and impulses. All of us have probably read accounts of misguided individuals who did foolish and even terrible things under the belief that God was guiding them.

Four Ways to Assess Spiritual Guidance

We can learn to assess our Higher Power's guidance in the following ways:

1. It will always be highly moral and will not involve harming ourselves or others.

2. It will strengthen and enhance our individual recoveries.

3. It can include helpful feedback or assistance from others, whether they seem to be spiritual or not.

4. It will usually be compatible with each individual's fundamental nature.

At times, this guidance can lead to results that can only be called uncommon and miraculous. Most of the time, however, our lives move along in patterns similar to the lives of others around us. For that matter, we should view all people as spiritual beings who are part of God's world, so our personal guidance is not a case of receiving favors or advantages that are not available on the same terms to everybody.

The most beneficial feature of this guidance can be in avoiding mistakes that could easily occur as a result of personal selfishness and a headstrong nature. Since we should also view sobriety as God's will for us, this alone spares any of us from a living death. When we face a major threat or an important decision, we can almost feel something kicking in to help us along after we have completely surrendered our will in the matter. Though the answers come through seemingly ordinary processes, we can also feel that these processes are divinely directed.

It's well understood that we humans have an amazing trick of being able to carry out selfish plans of our own while insisting that we are following God's will. Alcoholics and other victims of compulsive disorders can spot such hypocrisy on the part of certain religious people. Yet we can easily fall into the same trap ourselves in following the Twelve Steps.

There are many times, however, when our individual wants can be entirely in line with what appears to be the will of God. Everybody wants security, love, and happiness, for example, and these are apparently God-given desires that are part of our nature. But when we have tried to meet these needs in the wrong ways, trouble has come and brought us down. Most of the time, we do not need preachers and lecturers to tell us when our drives and actions do not reflect true spiritual guidance. The action, whatever it is, seems to carry its own built-in punishments or rewards.

Active alcoholism itself is a glaring example of seeking security and happiness in the wrong way. It's certainly not far-fetched to say that alcoholics think they've found a key to paradise when they discover alcohol. It soon turns out that this is a false belief and what seems to be paradise quickly becomes a living hell. This speaks for itself so loudly that no sane person could ever believe that it is the will of God for the alcoholic to keep on drinking. As for punishment, alcoholics bring enough upon themselves even without the eternal damnation that was warned about in the sermons and lectures of old.

Once sobriety is achieved, however, lots of other choices and decisions have to be made as we go about living our lives on the new basis. While it should be clear that sobriety is God's will for us, other choices and decisions can bring considerable turmoil and stress. We are told again and again to turn things over to our Higher Power or to let go and let God, but in practice this can be confusing. We can be faced with such questions as "Does God want me to take this new job?" or "Does God want me to be healed of this malady?" or "Does God want me to win this election or to get this promotion?"

There may also be others telling us what the will of God should be in our lives. AA's parent society, the Oxford Group, had a practice of seeking guidance for others. This brought positive benefits, as when Henrietta Seiberling was led to seek guidance for Dr. Bob in part of a process that eventually resulted in the founding of AA. But Bill W. later became critical of this type of guidance, as when a contingent of Oxford Group members said they had guidance that he should discontinue his work with alcoholics! Had he followed their advice, there would have been no AA or eventual recovery for millions.

What's important in all of this is that we must individually feel and know that what we're doing is within the will of

God for us, if we hope to release any matter. If we have doubt, fear, or guilt about a course of action, we probably will not get the strong conviction that our Higher Power is working along with us to reach our objectives. If we are certain, however, that our actions are in line with divine will, we'll be able to say, with great confidence, that "if God be for us, who can be against us?"

Always Moral

One approach in assessing spiritual guidance is to know that true guidance will always be highly moral and will not involve harming ourselves or others. This immediately rules out any actions by which somebody is going to be harmed through a sin of omission or commission on our part.

As an example, we may find ourselves in a transaction that will give us a great advantage over another who has been misled or fails to understand just what is involved in the bargain. Perhaps it is the sale of a house or an automobile with serious hidden defects or problems that we have not disclosed.

We could easily rationalize our actions by insisting that it's the other person's responsibility to discover such problems. Many people do make such rationalizations and continue to be respected members of their communities. But we cannot take this position and still continue with the feeling that we are releasing our will and lives to God's care and keeping. It is necessary to remember that the person with whom we're dealing also has equal rights under God and must receive fair treatment. If we violate this rule, it will come back to haunt us in some way. Harsh, tricky treatment of others will always interfere with our conscious contact with God as we understand Him. There's no need to quote Bible verses or seek intellectual proofs of this reality. Our own experience and the experiences of friends will supply sufficient proof, if we will learn from it.

The wise course is always to follow the moral way that is implied in the Twelve Step program. Tell the truth, be honest, and let the outcome be whatever God wills it to be. Even if this course seems to result in some personal loss, the real gain is much more important. You will have a clear conscience and you will also find a strengthened ability to believe that God is living and working in your life.

What about those people who commit terrible acts because God "told them to"? This is never true guidance. It is always an attempt to avoid responsibility for one's own anger-driven actions. Even if the individuals profess to be religious, they are not really carrying out God's will. They are only acting under the fierce passions that have bedeviled humankind ever since the dawn of history.

Strengthening Recovery

Any guidance we receive and actions we take must also strengthen and enhance our individual recoveries. If an action is somehow wrong or threatening to our recovery, we have to question whether it is the will of God for us.

In one case, for example, a young woman stated at a meeting that she could not return to the nursing profession because the ready availability of drugs had proved to be her downfall on several occasions. She felt that she needed to get into a line of work that did not include this unusual type of temptation.

Another member immediately began to argue with her, insisting that true recovery should include the ability to work in an environment where drugs were present. He cited the example of some AA members who work as bartenders or attend many business functions where liquor is served. People shouldn't have to shield themselves from such temptations, he believed.

But he was clearly overstepping proper boundaries in giving such advice. While it is true that some members stay clean and sober while working around liquor and drugs, others may not have the confidence or spiritual strength to do this. We cannot say what every person should do at any point in recovery. It is always wise, however, to provide as safe a margin as possible to ensure recovery.

Including Feedback from Others

"Letting go and letting God" can also include helpful feedback or assistance from others, whether they seem to be spiritual or not. We should always be ready to accept any information from human sources as part of God's guidance if it seems to be right and just.

There's an old story about a doubting person who declared that getting God's guidance didn't work because of an experience he had while lost in the north woods of Canada. "I prayed for help, but God didn't answer my prayers," he explained.

Another person, hearing the statement, said, "Well, something must have happened, or you wouldn't be here to tell about it."

The doubting person's reply: "Right! If that guide hadn't come along when he did to help me, I'd still be up there!"

That's our experience in seeking guidance. Our help and answers can come through many channels, depending on the need of the moment. While these answers seem ordinary and coincidental, we strengthen our spiritual resources when we learn to look upon them as God-directed. It should also be humbling to reflect that some of our most important help may even come from individuals who are menial and lowly in the world's view. The Twelve Step movement, in fact, has many individuals who are brilliant examples in practicing the program but are not considered outstanding performers as measured by worldly success standards.

The other side of this idea is that we, too, can become channels in helping others or giving them the information they need. The wonder of Twelve Step discussion meetings is that many thoughts and opinions are thrown out on the table, to be picked up and digested by whoever might need or want them at the moment. The person who shares at meetings may often be astonished by the number of people who say they received just what they needed at that special time.

Compatible with Our Fundamental Nature

It's not uncommon to hear people say that they feared seeking God's guidance because they might be ordered to do some sacrificial thing such as becoming a missionary in a remote country. In other cases, there are fears that God will order us into dreary lives of obedience and poverty.

While it's apparently true that some people do feel guided into such callings, real guidance will not work that way for most of us. Within reason, we can expect it to be something that is usually compatible with our own fundamental nature and aptitudes. It should be obvious, for example, that no person will become a self-sacrificing missionary without at least having inclinations along that line. It is also doubtful that God, the author of everything that exists, will direct us into actions for which we are unsuited. What is most likely to happen under guidance is that we will be led into activities that best utilize our past training, aptitudes, and intelligence. This was particularly true in the case of Bill W., the cofounder of Alcoholics Anonymous. Though he had training in electrical engineering and law, he became a stockbroker during the hectic 1920s, when the great bull market was roaring to its crest on Wall Street. This field also fitted another characteristic in his personality: He was not the sort of person who adapted well to a conventional job or ordered responsibilities, and this position gave him immense freedom and latitude, which proved to be disastrous in his drinking.

Yet all of Bill's previous training, aptitudes, and traits, along with his communication skills, became valuable in the formation of AA. His engineering training gave him knowledge of the importance of principles; his legal studies aided him in setting up various guidelines for AA; and his business experience gave him a balanced view of how things ought to work in human relationships. As for his resistance to steady, organized work, this, too, was an asset for AA. From 1938 onward, he devoted all of his attention to AA matters, at a time when this was most needed by the fellowship. Everybody benefited far more from this work of Bill's than if he had gone into a business career and faded from the AA scene.

Each of us has aptitudes, experience, and interests that can be a useful part of the world's activities. Under the lash of alcoholism and other compulsions, most of us missed out on our true calling and overlooked other opportunities that should have been ours. But when we practice "letting go and letting God," we will not be led astray if true guidance is coming through. More likely than not, we will be led in astonishing ways into activities that are just right for us and just right for others. There is no need to fret about how this is supposed to happen. It usually comes about in ways that we couldn't have foreseen or planned.

We must be wary, however, of being misled by our own wishful thinking and unrealistic desires. One person, for example, subscribed to a confidence-building program that did wonders in helping him overcome shyness and reticence. He became so enthusiastic about confidence-building that he neglected the clients from his regular work and spent most of his time selling the inspirational program that had helped him. This soon fizzled out, however, and before long he had returned to his original work and was soon performing at a higher level of success.

What was the lesson in this experience? It is that God can lead us into better uses of our talents and time, but we do not have to become missionaries in the process. Our friend's true work was not to be a missionary of confidence-building but to apply his new confidence and higher inspiration in his regular work, for which he was extremely gifted. All of us need confidence and inspiration, but the world is not so ordered that we can neglect the basic talents and experience we have already.

In Twelve Step meetings, we will hear numerous accounts from people who have practiced "letting go and letting God" in dealing with various problems and needs in their lives. We will not necessarily agree with all of these personal stories, and some may even appear bizarre and misleading. If we listen carefully, though, we will hear a number of accounts that are convincing and true. These shared stories can help us learn and grow as we continue to practice what it really means to "let go and let God."

It's always helpful to review the ways guidance has worked in our own lives and the lives of friends. One AA member, for example, had been unemployed for a long time and was becoming discouraged. He had been promised a good job with a Manhattan firm, but the actual hiring was delayed. Feeling frustrated after another futile trip to the company, he took the subway home. For some reason, he took a different subway from the one he usually traveled. Riding in the same car was an old friend he hadn't seen in months. The friend steered him to a wonderful new job opportunity that gave him satisfactory employment for a number of years.

Was this God's guidance or just plain coincidence and luck? AA friends often tell us that there's no such thing as coincidence—God is running everything, whether we want to believe it or not. But if it's simply luck that is calling the shots, it will always be better if we're sober and doing our part. Maybe "letting go" simply means giving up the idea that we're victims of blind chance. And "letting God" may simply mean acknowledging and accepting a guidance and a power that have been there all along.

Came to Believe

When we surrendered to our Higher Power, the journey began. Many of us had trouble believing that a God existed when we began our recovery program, because for years we thought we were the masters of our own affairs. We paid attention to no desires or wishes but our own.

When we realized how much help we needed, we first looked to other members and our group for support. By rejecting at first the idea of a Power higher than ourselves, many of us did not accept the idea of a Power other than ourselves. As we have made spiritual progress, most of us now have a clear and ongoing belief in a Higher Power that we choose to call God.

It's important to our recovery to rely on our Higher Power, as our own belief in a Higher Power is what can and does save us from our addiction. Only two of the Steps talk about addiction. The other ten talk about spiritual growth. We have a firm foundation for spiritual health and spiritual progress when we continue to believe in our Higher Power.

Accepting Guidance:
Stop Struggling with God

We listened to a qualification the other night at an AA meeting that was devoted to the Third Step, and we realized that for many of us much time must pass before we can say in simple confidence, "The Lord is my shepherd. I shall not want."

The great psalm of David is indeed a song of simple faith, which only those who do not struggle against the Supreme Power can sing.

Why do we struggle? Perhaps fear and worry cloud our vision and make us unwilling to let ourselves go. More likely, our faith is pride, which short-circuits our reason or else sends our minds into winding by-paths of involved thinking. With pride goes a quarrelsome spirit, which short-circuits the mind. Selfishness, too, blinds the vision and hides the path.

Some of us struggle not against the Supreme Power but with it. The harder we try to understand, the less we do understand. Success comes then when we quit struggling, when we relax and let ourselves see what there is to be seen.

Only a few of us, a very few of us, ever have a dramatic revelation of the existence of a Higher Power. Such revelations usually result from intensely emotional experiences. For most of us, there are no shafts of light, no voices in the sky, no seizures.

The Supreme Power reveals itself to us as we permit God to do so. But we who have sat so long in the seat of the scornful and walked in the paths of the ungodly do have to seek the Supreme Power and we do have to ask for guidance without mental reservation. The Supreme Power may be admitted to a mind cluttered with rubbish, since a beginning has to be made, but it will not abide in a mind that devotes itself to rubbish. Weeds will choke good seed, and all the more so if we continue to encourage the weeds.

First we have to seek. We may start by setting aside a part of each day for a period of quiet thought. Let us be alone, at such times, and let us set aside all contention, all fuming, all fretting. The first necessity is to quiet the mind, to shut out all thought until relaxation comes. If we get no further than this at first, the mental quiet will help.

The next thing is to let the mind reach out, until it can find something upon which it can rest. For some of us, that something is the endless space that makes us feel the vastness of the universe. Some of us demand something more concrete and some demand an actual object of some sort, something inanimate or something of human form whose goodness and virtue we respect.

The Power that we seek is the source of all good; from it comes nothing evil. The Power is a strict judge of our honesty, of our acts. When we hold mental conversation with the Supreme Power, we are brought to the line of absolute truth. Every evasion delays our finding rest, delays our finding the path to a new way of life. For those who continue to sit in the seat of the scornful, there is no help in AA. But those who will look for the help of a Higher Power will find it. Realization may come slowly at first, but it will come. We learn, step by step, to accept the guidance of the Supreme Power.

Chapter Five
One Day at a Time
(Reduction)

Here's a recovering person's view of the way "one day at a time" was practiced during the worst of his drinking:

> In my drinking days, I took considerable solace in having enough money or liquor for that day's drinking. It didn't seem to matter that tomorrow I would be broke and horribly sick. That pain in the immediate future was blotted out by the dubious comfort of being able to drink here and now.
>
> Of course I can see today that this was a sick attitude. But strangely enough, the same idea has served me well in sobriety: If I focus on today, or perhaps whatever I'm doing here and now, things always go better.

A Drinking Idea Is Recycled
for Healthy Purposes

This is an interesting idea—that alcoholics are practicing "one day at a time" while they are drinking. But it seems to be true. Compulsive people apparently have a desperate need to eliminate the pain and stress of yesterday and tomorrow and to bring the focus down to the current moment. This is terribly sick, but in recovery we can do the same thing in a healthy way.

Some people say that this is unrealistic. After all, as human beings, we have to think long-term as well as short-term. If we just give our attention to the needs of today, what about the future?

"One day at a time" does not mean that we blot out future concerns. Indeed, one of today's responsibilities might be planning for something that's to take place next week or next year. What this slogan does mean is that we do not clutter up our minds and feelings with too many things at one time. We deal with the matters that have first claim on our attention, and then we take up other matters as they become important. The main focus of our attention is always on what we can do here and now rather than what lies down the road or can be dealt with only in the days ahead.

Living in the Present Both Practically and Spiritually

The slogan "one day at a time" also must be applied in a broader way if we're to have true serenity: We must close the door on the past and refuse to fear the future. Again and again, recovering people discover that when they're failing to be effective in what they're doing today, it's either because they're borrowing trouble from the past or worrying about their ability to meet future problems. Human beings are not able to carry such burdens for long. There's little doubt that many of our difficulties, even in sobriety, would have been much easier to face if we hadn't been living in either the past or the future.

Yet another application of "one day at a time" is in carrying out the basic purpose of a Twelve Step program. Today, for this twenty-four-hour period, we can be free from our compulsion, whatever it is. We can always have such freedom for at least one day. As an older AA member would say to struggling newcomers, "You can stay sober a day at a time, or even five minutes at a time, if necessary. If you were in jail, you'd have to stay sober and it wouldn't kill you."

As a spiritual idea, "one day at a time" is virtually repeated in the prayer that closes most Twelve Step meetings: "Give us this day our daily bread." In his book *The Sermon on the Mount,* Emmet Fox states that *bread* stands for anything that's necessary for our daily living.

You'll find the same day-at-a-time approach in the Bible's Sermon on the Mount, which in one version states, "So do not worry about tomorrow, for tomorrow will have worries of its own. Let each day be content with its own ills."[1]

Famous People Who Lived One Day at a Time

It is also reassuring that "one day at a time" has worked so well for prominent people in the past. It was reportedly a turning point for Sir William Osler when he discovered, in the writings of Thomas Carlyle, these words: "Our main business is not to see what lies dimly at a distance, but to do

---

1. J. M. Powis Smith and Edgar J. Goodspeed, *The Bible: An American Translation* (Chicago: The University of Chicago Press, 1931), 9.

what lies clearly at hand." Osler, who became the most famous physician of his day and helped transform Johns Hopkins University into a leading medical school, became an advocate of living in day-tight compartments. Osler even insisted that he had no special quality of brains but that he succeeded by concentrating on doing today's work superbly today.

According to Dale Carnegie, Osler kept on his desk a poem by the Indian dramatist and poet Kālidāsa. It sums up the whole idea of living one day at a time:

Look to this day!
For it is life, the very life of life.
In its brief course
Lie all the verities and realities of your existence:
The bliss of growth
The glory of action
The splendor of beauty,
For yesterday is but a dream
And tomorrow is only a vision,
But today well lived makes every yesterday a dream of happiness
And every tomorrow a vision of hope,
Look well, therefore, to this day!
Such is the salutation to the dawn.

Today Is the Now

I've shut the door on yesterday
And thrown the key away.
Tomorrow holds no fears for me
Since I have found today.
—Vivian Y. Laramore

Living in the now is one of the most important ways of finding lasting recovery. One of the favorite slogans to be followed is "one day at a time." We willingly accept that yesterday is gone forever and tomorrow is only an expectation. When we have finished with yesterday and have no fear of tomorrow, we can be assured that we can truly be content with each new today.

Living in the now is an acceptance of life's realities. Honesty is the keynote to being happy throughout each day as it comes. Today surely is the "first day of the rest of our lives." It can be, if lived with gratitude, love, and honesty, the best day yet in our newly found today.

Today truly can be that wonderful exciting day that on yesterday I eagerly called "tomorrow." I can greet every today by exclaiming, "This day can be the start of the best years of my life."

What Is the Problem?

Alcoholics and other compulsive people are usually intelligent persons who understand the necessity for living a day at a time. Knowing this and putting it into practice are different matters, however, and often takes more than the frequent repetition of a helpful slogan. If we're unable to bring our focus down to the current moment, it might help to decide what the problem is—what's keeping us from doing what we know should be done.

One barrier is our inability to be satisfied with the humdrum, sometimes boring lives most people have. We may feel that we're faced with boring work, dull people, and drab and colorless surroundings. We hit snags in our work or find that our performance is way below our expectations of perfection. There is a strong yearning for excitement, for something that will take us out of ourselves and fill us with the energy and enchantment we seek and feel we deserve. This boredom also makes us lazy and inefficient, which in turn leads to further boredom.

Under those circumstances, we can easily crave excitement in the form of drinking or other compulsive behaviors. This is treacherous and destructive, but it's part of the mechanism of compulsion. Again and again at AA meetings, alcoholics have described their insane flight from boredom. We fled boredom only to be plunged into situations that brought more boredom, while the excitement we craved proved to be false and fleeting. Our answer comes in facing that we have been bored and lazy, while deciding that we must deal with it in a constructive way. We should use whatever positive aids we can find to help us in this search. It may require taking our own inventory with another understanding person, but it must be done if we are to survive and grow in the Twelve Step program.

Practicing gratitude can be a useful tool in this search. It's not unusual to find people who are bored and resentful about situations that others enjoy and appreciate. If we resent the work that we are required to do, we may actually be creating our own forms of boredom. But if we turn it around and remember to be grateful for our employment and income, we may also discover that things weren't as boring as we thought they were. The grateful person is likely to reach that state of mind, while the dissatisfied and lazy will only find things to criticize about every situation they find themselves in. It is literally true that sick alcoholics are usually trying to escape from wherever they are in both place and time!

The Burdens of Fear and Worry

Fear and worry are additional problems that cut into our ability to live "one day at a time." While most fears and worries appear as legitimate concerns, they are usually more like bad habits that some of us acquire so early in life that we don't even understand how unnecessary they are. If we were truly honest, most of us would admit that many of our fears and worries are unrelated to the things that seem to be causing them; when certain problems or threats are removed from our lives, we tend to find new things to fear or fret over. It is also true that we have a difficult time remembering what we were worrying about last month or last year.

When this is pointed out, however, we're likely to come to our own defense by pointing out that we should fear real threats and we ought to be concerned about serious problems in our lives. We might say that fear helps us avoid danger, while reasonable worry prods us to take needed action to deal with the issues that are causing us to worry.

This explanation sounds plausible, but it takes no account of how fear and worry rob us of the time and energy we should spend on today's problems. Far from causing us to act in our own behalf, fear and worry can actually paralyze us so that no action is taken at all. The greater the fear and the more intense the worry, the more likely it is that we'll become so indecisive and timid that we do nothing. By rehearsing all the troubles that might come to us now—or those we've had in the past—we can bring on the very conditions we've tried to avoid: The thing I greatly feared has come upon me!

"One day at a time" can be a useful guide for people who must deal with continuous fears and worries. For one thing, the slogan serves as a reminder that we're empowered to deal with the matters we can handle here and now only. We should take the approach of the business owner who was warned that the general economy was heading for the falls. His reply was, "We might be heading for the falls, but I'll still be paddling when we go over." In effect, he was saying that he wasn't going to quit and resign himself to fate simply because future problems might overwhelm him despite his best efforts.

People in recovery can refocus their lives by taking the same approach. No matter what has happened in the past or might happen in the future, we have the power to do our best today, wherever we are and whatever we're doing. The Twelve Step programs are aimed at clearing away the wreckage of the past—at neither regretting the past nor fearing the future. We can make surprising progress when we keep that in mind.

What often happens, of course, is that our Higher Power guides us into activities that eventually surpass anything we could have imagined for ourselves. One of the early AA members in Detroit, for example, lost a fine position during the final stages of his drinking. It was a particularly humiliating experience and he was required to clean out his desk and leave in the full view of the office staff. The experience filled him with rage and a desire to get even, as well as regret over the loss of a splendid job and salary.

He started a small shop that was soon failing because of his continuing drinking. Then he found the AA program and underwent a vast change in his thinking. He accepted responsibility for his past problems and even found an opportunity to shake hands with the man who had subjected him to such gratuitous humiliation. He also began to concentrate on rescuing his own business, small as it was.

The business prospered, and he became wealthy as well as a highly admired AA member. While he was not a person to gloat over his material success, one could reflect that he was actually better off than if he had not lost the earlier position! By releasing the past and forgiving himself and others, he was able to build a future that was far brighter than anything he could have dreamed for himself.

No Regrets

Of all sad words of tongue or pen, the saddest are these,
"It might have been."

—Whittier

Unless we live in the now, *we are in danger of suffering the agony of regret. We can't spend all our time thinking "life's not fair." We cannot afford to excuse everything with "what ifs." We used those words constantly during the years we wasted on obeying compulsions we knew could destroy us.*

We remember the years before recovery and accept them as objective lessons of what it could be like again if we become careless or complacent. But we don't regret them. Regret only leads to depression and perhaps a return to active addiction.

We must stop dwelling on the impossibility of undoing the wrongs of yesterday. Instead, we must begin enjoying the "right things" that are now possible in recovery.

It is impossible to relive my past. I can create a good past now only by living this day the best way I can, so that tomorrow I can look back without having to say "It might have been."

Pessimism and Low Self-Confidence

Rightly applied, "one day at a time" can also help in surmounting the severe limitations of pessimism and low self-confidence, traits that seem to go hand in hand. An old saying has it that a pessimist is one who sees a glass as half-empty, while the optimist views it as half-full. The pessimist, in other words, looks upon life as a process of losing, while the optimist thinks of it in terms of gaining.

Most alcoholics, it turns out, have been both pessimists and optimists while drinking. In drinking, however, neither pessimism nor optimism is helpful—the pessimism is too severe, while the optimism is completely unrealistic. In sobriety, we can change all that by focusing only on today's problems and concerns. If we try to run a balance sheet on the past or projections for the future, we can become lost in pessimism, feeling that there's been too much loss that can never be reversed in the future.

That changes if we look only at today and what should be measured as success. We're gaining and succeeding today if we stay sober, free of our compulsion for this twenty-four-hour period. We're also gaining if we work productively today, even if it's in an activity that seems to be far below our talents and expectations. We're gaining if we avoid foolish arguments, loss of temper, or miserable reflections about the past. We're gaining if we feel the development of a closer contact with our Higher Power, experience that will help us as we strive for such contacts in the future.

On that path, our self-confidence will also improve. People who believe they are seeking and carrying out God's will generally go about their affairs with more confidence than if they lacked that conviction. If we believe in God as the author of justice and love, with a true interest in creating a better world, we'll find astonishing improvements taking place in our own lives. As for regretting the past, we'll have the more positive attitude of viewing it as a price that had to be paid for finding the Twelve Step program. As for fearing the future, we'll eliminate that because of our trust that God has a wonderful future in mind for us. In the best sense of those terms, we'll be optimists with bursting confidence that the future will exceed our greatest hopes.

A Tool for One Day at a Time

It is never easy to follow a one-day-at-a-time program, although life does become easier when one learns how to do it. There are many pitfalls along the way, however, and even the AA practice of leading at meetings can have the unintended consequences of recalling the mistakes and bitterness of the past. We can also work ourselves into an unsettled state by fretting over the problems in society and the world, to say nothing of our own troubles.

One handy tool for navigating life's troubled waters appeared in AA's early meetings. It was a series of statements entitled "Just for Today," and it has been reprinted numerous times apparently without author attribution or any identification as to its source. Though it is not a part of AA literature, it has been reproduced by the Al-Anon Family Group Headquarters. The series serves as a good summation of living one day at a time:

> Just for today I will try to live through this day only and not tackle all my problems at once. I can do something for twelve hours that would appall me if I felt that I had to keep it up for a lifetime.
>
> Just for today I will be happy. This assumes to be true what Abraham Lincoln said, that "Most folks are as happy as they make up their minds to be."
>
> Just for today I will adjust myself to what is and not try to adjust everything to my own desires. I will take my luck as it comes and fit myself to it.
>
> Just for today I will try to strengthen my mind. I will study. I will learn something useful. I will not be a mental

loafer. I will read something that requires effort, thought, and concentration.

Just for today I will exercise my soul in three ways: I will do somebody a good turn and not get found out; if anybody knows of it, it will not count. I will do at least two things I don't want to do—just for exercise. I will not show anyone that my feelings are hurt; they may be hurt, but today I will not show it.

Just for today I will be agreeable. I will look as well as I can, dress becomingly, keep my voice low, be courteous, criticize not one bit. I won't find fault with anything, nor will I try to improve or regulate anybody but myself.

Just for today I will have a program. I may not follow it exactly, but I will have it. I will save myself from two pests: hurry and indecision.

Just for today I will have a quiet half hour all by myself, and relax. During this half hour, sometime, I will try to get a better perspective of my life.

Just for today I will be unafraid. Especially I will not be afraid to enjoy what is beautiful and to believe that as I give to the world, so the world will give to me.

Chapter Six
Pass It On
(Service)

'Pass It On,' the title of Bill W.'s biography, was also his answer to people who would all but overwhelm him with their gratitude. The AA cofounder made it clear that the best way to express any thanks is to pass the message on to others or, as he liked to say, "the million who still don't know."

"Pass it on" is more than a mere saying. It expresses a principle that lies behind AA's remarkable growth and ability to survive as a fellowship. Without a built-in process of passing along its message, AA would soon wither and die. That's something any member can easily understand by observing the makeup of a single AA group over a span of four or five years. Each group usually undergoes a process of continuous change in membership during that period and probably would become inactive without the influx of new members as older ones leave or die.

The Secret of Individual Sobriety
and Fellowship Survival

But this necessity of passing it on is not always well understood, even within the fellowship. It is even less understood by people outside of AA. Here's how one member recalls his personal experience with it:

A funny thing happened during my first year of sobriety. Some dear family members became critical of my attendance at AA meetings. I heard what many recovering persons hear after an initial pattern of sobriety has been established. They would say to me, "You're sober now. Why on earth do you keep going to those meetings and associating with those people?"

What made this sort of comment more irksome was that my relatives gave as an example another person who didn't attend meetings anymore. He had gone to St. Thomas Hospital in Akron, Ohio, where Dr. Bob and others had helped set him on a sober path. Now he was getting along just fine without those meetings and those people! And the implied question was "Why can't you do the same?"

The member agreed that any member has the right to choose whether or not he or she attends meetings:

I've seen many people stay sober without meetings, though I've also seen people whose relapses probably began when they dropped meeting attendance.

I have two good reasons for my own group participation and meeting attendance. One is that I view it as an excellent way to stay close to the program to maintain my own sobriety. The second reason is that meeting attendance is the best way to pass on to others what I've learned.

I am the only person who can share my experience with others, for whatever it's worth. Discussion and speaker meetings are the best forums for this on a regular basis. I can usually be assured that every meeting will include persons at all levels of recovery. We go to learn and we go to share.

I don't know if the person my relatives cited continued to stay sober. Even if he did, he may have been denying himself opportunities for personal growth. If he wished to pass on what he had learned from his time with Dr. Bob, the meetings would have been the best place to meet others with the same problems.

There's also the matter of maintaining the fellowship as a future source of help for others. It probably would have been unkind to ask him how his recovery could have come about if Dr. Bob and the early pioneers had not seen the need to pass it on. Now that hindsight gives us such a sweeping view of the past, we can easily see that the future recovery of thousands hinged on these pioneers staying on course and accepting what they viewed as a moral obligation to help others.

This member's comments certainly carry meaning for us. It's possible that the day may come when millions of people in Twelve Step groups of all kinds will acknowledge a debt to the work of these AA pioneers. Dr. Bob had no such lofty vision of changing the world, but he did explain his own view on the subject. "I spend a great deal of time passing on what I learned to others who want and need it badly," he wrote in his Big Book personal story. "I do it for four reasons:

1. Sense of duty.

2. It is a pleasure.

3. Because in so doing I am paying my debt to the man who took time to pass it on to me.

4. Because every time I do it I take out a little more insurance for myself against a possible slip."[1]

How Passing It On Became an AA Principle

The principle of sharing one's experience with others—and thus helping them in the process—is so much a part of the Twelve Step program that members now take it for granted. Yet there was nothing in AA's early experience that made it inevitable that this principle be accepted and followed. Much of it was borrowed from AA's predecessor society, the Oxford Group, and a large share of it grew out of the thoughts and feelings of the two AA cofounders, Bill W. and Dr. Bob.

Bill W.'s personal recollection of how the principle came to him is carried in his personal story in AA's text, *Alcoholics Anonymous.* In this account, Bill outlined the horror and defeat of his drinking experiences and then told how an old drinking friend showed up sober to discuss a program of recovery he had found in the Oxford Group. Though at first resistant, Bill accepted this program and subsequently underwent an astonishing spiritual experience that changed his life. He described the thoughts that followed:

While I lay in the hospital the thought came that there were thousands of hopeless alcoholics who might be

---

1. *Alcoholics Anonymous,* 3d ed. (New York: AA World Services, 1976), 180–81.

glad to have what had been so freely given me. Perhaps I could help some of them. They in turn might work with others.

My friend had emphasized the absolute necessity of demonstrating these principles in all my affairs. Particularly it was imperative to work with others as he had worked with me. Faith without works was dead, he said. And how appallingly true for the alcoholic! For if an alcoholic failed to perfect and enlarge his spiritual life through work and self-sacrifice for others, he could not survive the certain trials and low spots ahead. If he did not work, he would surely drink again, and if he drank, he would surely die. Then faith would be dead indeed. With us it is just like that.[2]

This idea went through a number of changes before it emerged as AA's Twelfth Step. Bill W., early in his sobriety, discovered that working with others often saved the day for himself, though he had no success in helping other alcoholics find sobriety. But the magic day came when he met Dr. Bob Smith in Akron, Ohio, and within weeks a new band of recovering alcoholics was beginning to develop. Everybody seemed to accept the belief that passing it on was necessary.

---

2. *Alcoholics Anonymous*, 14–15.

An Oxford Group Idea

"Passing it on" is an idea AA inherited from the Oxford Group, the spiritual fellowship that helped AA's founders find sobriety. There is some irony in this, because some Oxford Group members soon tried to dissuade Bill W. from carrying out his single-minded effort to help other drunks. Nonetheless, Oxford Group members worked assertively to win others over to their program.

Frank Buchman, the Oxford Group founder, called this activity "continuance," a process of one changed person seeking to change others. It was this feature of the Oxford Group program that impelled Ebby T., an old school friend, to call on Bill W. and offer the plan to him. Not surprisingly, Ebby had learned this principle from other Oxford Group members who had helped him. While AA is indebted to the Oxford Group for this important practice, it's important to know that AA modified the practice to meet the needs of the recovering alcoholic. In the view of the AA cofounders, alcoholics needed a special approach as well as a steady commitment to the single goal of staying sober and helping others find sobriety. The Oxford Group leaders, however, were opposed to this idea and to suggestions that separate divisions should be set up within their fellowship for helping alcoholics. This strong difference of opinion helped bring about a separation of the alcoholics from the Oxford Group.

One change the AA members made was to tone down what they thought was the excessive evangelism practiced by the Oxford Group. Bill W.'s views on this are set forth in his biography: "The principle of aggressive evangelism so prominent as an Oxford Group attitude had to be dropped in order to get any result with alcoholics," he wrote in a 1940 letter. "Experience showed that this principle, which may have been absolutely vital to the success of the Oxford Group, would seldom touch neurotics of our hue."[3]

Though the AA message is not passed on aggressively, it is still deeply understood in the fellowship that it must be passed on if alcoholics are to find and maintain sobriety in the fellowship. This passing on usually takes place through contacts between AA members and meeting discussions and talks, with members explaining what happened to them and how they were helped to a new way of life.

A Principle for Human Progress—or Destruction

Like many principles that apply to human affairs, "pass it on" can work either for our advancement or our destruction. It is well understood that most of the bad ideas and practices in the world have been passed on by previous generations. To our sorrow, we suffer today from the fear and anger that have been passed down by many generations. In drinking, we may have passed on some bad ideas and practices of our own, to the detriment of family and friends. It's widely believed now, for example, that children of alcoholics carry deep emotional scars from their childhood that affect their behavior later on.

What this tells us is that we'll always be passing our own beliefs and actions on to others, whether good or bad. For this reason, we can be grateful that the Twelve Step program

---

3.   '*Pass It On*' (New York: AA World Services, 1984), 172.

gives us the opportunity to pass on constructive thoughts and actions rather than the harmful ones from the half-world of alcoholism. If we do this in the right way and for the right reasons, we can be a positive and uplifting influence not only on family and friends, but also on people we've never met and who will never meet us.

Proof of this is all around us, but we can find our best example simply by looking at what's happened in AA. First, the fellowship was launched in 1935 using ancient principles that had been passed on through the centuries. The founders of AA passed on their own experience, which was then given to individual members who established groups. Most of these people are no longer with us, but their legacy is alive and growing and is benefiting people who probably weren't even born when the pioneering work was being done. These people, in turn, will pass the legacy on to others—a rich endowment that could last for centuries in different forms.

While this fine work is going on, other ideas and practices are causing the destruction of individuals, societies, and nations. We have no answer for this folly, but we can at least be grateful that God has enabled us to be part of the solution to human distress rather than causing more of it, as we did in ignorance while drinking. Passing it on is not only a duty for recovering alcoholics. It is also a wonderful privilege.

Benefiting Both Parties

How do we help another person?

The world overflows with schemes for changing individuals and societies so that human lives can finally be free from misery, poverty, violence, pain, and sickness. Unfortunately, most such schemes either never are tried or fail to bring promised results after being put into practice. Quite often, the people who are targeted as needing help may be the ones most resistant to any plans for change.

That certainly seems to be true of alcoholics. Almost everybody agrees that alcoholism and other substance abuse are among the worst evils in society. Alcoholics are also deemed to be sick people in great need of help. Why can't this need be matched up with the resources—such as AA—that are known to work in helping alcoholics achieve sobriety?

AA members know and understand the reason why such a match cannot be easily made. "AA is not for those who need it, but for those who want it." This is a wise thought one frequently hears expressed at meetings. No program of recovery, AA included, is thought to show much promise unless the individual wants it and cooperates in personal recovery.

One factor, however, probably does give AA an advantage in carrying its message to those who still suffer. This advantage is in the personal attitude that's likely to be displayed by the people who acknowledge that they carry the message for their own benefit and not primarily to help the other person at all costs. This attitude should help to create a bond between the person carrying the message and the one needing help. It says, "I am doing this because I need to do it for my own good," not the more demeaning, "I am doing this because I have superior ideas that you must learn from me!"

There is, too, a great secret in helping anybody for your own benefit. The secret is that you are automatically rewarded whether or not the other person is helped. Every act of carrying the message is therefore successful, since somebody is helped in the process.

Action Proving the Principle

Any principle usually has to be demonstrated to be proved. This is particularly true in AA. People can have all sorts of beliefs about the way the program should work, but putting them into action proves their real merits.

Passing it on has done that in AA. There has truly been something close to magic in the way hopeless drunks have recovered and then become powerful advocates for the recovery of others. In some periods AA has grown almost by geometric progression, with membership doubling in size in a few months or years.

What is it that has been passed on? Most of the time, it has been experience, strength, and hope, the three time-tested qualities that are mentioned at almost every AA meeting. The experience is personal, but it embraces the Twelve Steps and all the related information that has been accumulated in AA. Members share their own experience in living a Twelve Step program and in dealing with the conflicts and problems of life. The strength is what each person acquires in living sober, and it includes the great spiritual resources that are at work in AA. And finally there's hope, the sort of optimism that keeps human beings going even in the face of overwhelming adversity.

Give with Humility

*The greatest pleasure I know is to do a good act in secret
and have it found out by accident.*
—Anonymous

*One bit of advice is given in many ways to those of us in
recovery. It is that we should give to others without looking
for any credit for our generosity. To give something for the
sheer joy of giving is the strongest step we can take in
achieving the humility that is so vital to us. Humility is
essential to our spiritual progress, and our spiritual progress
is a necessary part of our recovery.*

*The encouragement to serve without seeking praise comes
to us in many forms and many places. Ancient wisdom
advises us not to let our right hand know what our left
hand is doing, and not to "sound a trumpet" to announce
a good deed.*

Let me learn to give without seeking credit. This is a
humble act. It will result in the uplifting reward of
humility which is vital to my spiritual growth.

A Selfish Program

*A person shows their true self by
how much they need other people.*
—Anonymous

What giving we have discovered in our fellowship! From the very first meeting, we received an outstretched hand that offered us help. People gave freely and asked nothing in return. We, who had known so much taking, could hardly believe what we experienced. It just didn't seem real.

The reality is no put-on. There is a spirit of selfless fellowship in our program. But the truth is that those who are giving are also keeping. The gem they are holding on to is their recovery. Only those who give away what they have found can keep it.

Every time we share with another human being, we add something to our spiritual bank account, allowing us to draw on it when extra demands are made upon our courage. In the measure in which we share our burdens, they become lighter.

Imagine people saving their lives by giving them away! Oh, that I can only be so selfish!

Outlook of Two AA Members: A Question of Attitudes

Don D. went to an AA meeting one evening. He frowned when a member mispronounced a few words while reading "How It Works." He felt appalled when another member stood up and said he was an alcoholic and an addict. Another person talked too long. As he slipped out the door immediately after the meeting, Don D. muttered, "That was terrible. I should have stayed home."

Bob M. went to a meeting one evening. His head was bowed as he listened to the "Preamble" and "How It Works." His eyes moistened as he listened intently to a member tell his story. He was grateful for being able to attend this meeting. After cleanup and a little socializing, he paused, and as he locked the meeting room door, his thoughts were, "Thank God for such a beautiful fellowship."

Both AA members were at the same meeting. Each found what he was looking for.

Getting Out of Myself (Self-Pity)

The Fifth Promise tells me, "That feeling of uselessness and self-pity will disappear." I believe the Promises come as a direct result of action, and the Fifth Promise materialized through my involvement in service work.

I have a disease of self-obsession, selfishness, and self-centeredness. I became so wrapped up in how I felt, how I looked, and how I was doing that I never had time for you. It never dawned on me that you had troubles, that you had feelings, that you needed me. Even in recovery it is easy for me to slide into a state where I am the center of the universe.

Thank heaven for sponsors! I was steered toward service work from the start: setting up before and cleaning up after meetings. I could not understand how doing "silly" things like that was going to make me feel better. My problems needed "deeper" treatment. It didn't dawn on me until some time later that my sponsor, in her wisdom, knew that when I was involved in the makings of a meeting, I didn't have time to think about myself. Through this interaction, I became aware of others in this universe besides me.

It is impossible to reach out to another person and also feel useless. It is impossible to try to help another person and feel sorry for yourself at the same time. When I am reaching out, I don't have time to worry about myself. And when I am alone again, I usually can't remember what I was torn up about, or it just doesn't seem that bad anymore.

So the next time you feel mired in self-pity, ask yourself: "When was the last time I showed up at a meeting a half hour early? When did I chair last? Clean up? Have I volunteered recently? When did I last take a newcomer to a meeting?"

My Garden

I've been able to relate my recovery to a garden of beautiful flowers. Someone had planted the seeds, but it was up to me to surrender and begin the growing process (Step One). In this garden, I can see the beauty of the love, compassion, caring, and sharing with others.

The sun shines down with warmth to help me and my garden grow. I see this as my Higher Power (God) and love from my fellow members and my sponsor. Then the clouds roll in—this is my pain and sorrow, and from this rain (tears) and the storms of life, my garden and I grow and flourish. After the storms pass, the sun sparkles on the raindrops, and I know each time my H.P. is always there for me. In this I can find trust (Steps Two and Three). My flowers cannot grow without a little fertilizer—never too much, because then my flowers would burn up and die. Such would be my recovery.

Then there are weeds I need to keep clearing away by doing the Fourth and Fifth Steps. And by doing the Tenth Step daily I can try to keep the weeds of life from choking my beautiful flowers. The tools of the program help me, for without them I would have no suggested way to keep my garden in order.

The large weeds that are stubborn and hard to get rid of I keep plugging away at "one day at a time" with Steps Six and Seven. These are my defects of character. And to make amends without becoming self-righteous. This is all part of my growing process (Steps Eight and Nine). Prayer and meditation help nurture my garden every day (Step Eleven).

Then with time there come small seeds that are carried on the wind (voice and example) of my experience, strength, and hope of a better way of life to those who are suffering, in and out of recovery (Step Twelve).

Then perhaps another garden can grow and find the beauty, peace, and serenity that the fellowship promises if I am willing to practice these principles.

But if I choose to relapse, my garden becomes as if a nuclear bomb had struck, barren and with no life. For then I am lost.

Chapter Seven
Keep It Simple
(Simplification)

"Remember, Bill, let's not louse this thing up. Let's keep it simple!" I turned away, unable to say a word. That was the last time I ever saw him.[1]

So wrote Bill W. about his last meeting with Dr. Bob, the Akron physician who had been his partner in starting Alcoholics Anonymous. This recollection has since been enshrined in AA as Dr. Bob's final message to the fellowship: "Keep it simple."

A few months earlier, in Cleveland at AA's first international convention, Dr. Bob had stressed the simplicity of the program and added these immortal words: "Our Twelve Steps, when simmered down to the last, resolve themselves into the words *love* and *service*. We understand what love is, and we understand what service is. So let's bear those two things in mind."

---

1. *Alcoholics Anonymous Comes of Age* (New York: AA World Services, 1957), 214.

Remembering What's Important

Today, some AA members say that Bill W. was a power driver who would have complicated AA without Dr. Bob's firm insistence on simplicity. In fact, both men had a good understanding of the fundamentals that made the program work.

As a guide to living, "keep it simple" works not only in highlighting love and service as essentials of the program, but also in driving to the heart of any problem or issue.

An AA member who is also a writer says:

I've often thought of the idea of simplicity in connection with the large college library that I sometimes use for my research work. The library's one million volumes of material would be utter chaos without simple, logical coding systems for filing and retrieving them. In fact, the books themselves are all composed out of a mere twenty-six letters that are organized into words and sentences. We would never get anywhere in this great library without first understanding the alphabet and other keys to the system.

More on Bill W.'s Insights

This same simplicity should underlie all subjects that are otherwise complicated and mystifying. Bill W. reportedly gained much understanding from reading William James's *The Varieties of Religious Experience* while still a patient at New York's Towns Hospital in 1934. In this weighty and intricate book, Bill discovered three simple, common facts. These points are of major importance to Twelve Step programs. First, each of the personal cases described by James involved calamity; the individual had met complete defeat. Next, the defeat was admitted. Finally, there was an appeal to a Higher Power that resulted in victory out of defeat. Translated, all it says is this: We were licked, we admitted it, we asked God for help, and we found our answers. That's the great value of using "keep it simple" as a slogan: It reminds us of what's really essential in growth and recovery. Quite often, fretful demands for getting back to the basics are reflections of members' fears that essentials of love and service are being buried by other concerns.

As with most good ideas, there's a dark side to the use of this fine slogan. Wrongly understood, it can come out as "keep it simple-minded." This attitude conveys a false pride in being a recovering person while expressing contempt for professionals and others who are trying to understand the addiction field. Bill W. and Dr. Bob, though advocating simplicity, both had great admiration and gratitude for the highly educated professionals who were working in the field. They wanted more learning and understanding of alcoholism, not less.

There's plenty of experience to show that "keep it simple" can be a useful guide in all activities in addition to our own involvement in the Twelve Step program. Understanding any book or subject is always helped by grasping the basic theme and main ideas rather than becoming lost in the details. The slogan can also help in avoiding the trap of rambling in discussions and can provide an early warning system when others are rambling or missing the point. In looking at everything new, it can always help to look for the simple principles that are the key to understanding.

Twelve Ways to Learn the Program

One oft-repeated comment in AA is that it is a simple program for complicated people. This is a bit of a half-truth, because all people are complicated when you get to know more about them. What's closer to the mark is that alcoholics have a way of becoming confused about who they are and what they want in life. There are times when we may have taken a drink simply because we didn't know what to do next!

There are, however, simple ways to remember the essentials of the AA program and fellowship. One way—which still keeps it simple—is to number AA's simple ideas from one to twelve and to make a mental file for them. This is a system used by certain memory experts with astonishing results. Here's how it works for easy, simplified learning:

1. There is one simple purpose in AA: sobriety. This is the goal for both the individual and the AA society, and it is stated at every meeting. While other problems and needs often intrude, it is always important to keep this primary purpose out in front. It will always turn out to be a reliable beacon and guide no matter how stormy things might have become in our lives. It's safe to say that this emphasis on sobriety has helped keep AA on course as a world society.

2. Two simple words—*love* and *service*—should guide our actions, just as Dr. Bob stated in his last public talk. Love is a simple but profound feeling of goodwill that we can express unconditionally toward everybody and particularly toward those who may have hurt us.

Service is love in action and cannot be wrong or
misguided if the feeling that guides it is truly God-
inspired and God-directed.

3. There are three simple requirements for success in AA:
honesty, open-mindedness, and willingness. Often
simplified with the acronym *HOW,* these requirements
have stood the test of time. The key to it all is
willingness. If we have a burning desire to find
sobriety, we'll be willing to do anything necessary in
our search for it. Along the way, this willingness will
help us deal with our dishonesty and close-mindedness.

4. Four paradoxes are frequently mentioned in AA.
Written by John P., a professor at Kent State
University, these were introduced to the fellowship in
the second edition of *Alcoholics Anonymous,* which was
published in 1955.

It would be profitable for any AA member to track
down a second edition of the Big Book (the current
edition is the third) to study this short essay about
paradoxes, which begins on page 336 in a chapter
entitled "The Professor and the Paradox." The
professor, who almost destroyed his academic career
before finding sobriety, discovered four paradoxes of
how AA works. He defined a paradox as a statement that
is seemingly self-contradictory—that appears to be false
but that, upon careful examination, in certain instances
proves to be true. Here are four paradoxes of AA:

(We surrender to win.

(We give away to keep.

(We suffer to get well.

(We die to live.

Four, as a number, serves as a good memory device for other AA-related terms. Bill W., for example, sometimes mentioned the four horsemen of terror, bewilderment, frustration, and despair. There were also four standards (or "absolutes") practiced by the Oxford Group, AA's predecessor movement: love, honesty, unselfishness, and purity. Finally, it can also be beneficial in sobriety to reflect on the four cardinal virtues: temperance, prudence, justice, and fortitude.

5.   AA will answer five questions for you in time: Who am I? Why am I here? What is my purpose in life? Where is my place? When should I take action?

6.   If you're having a bad day, there are six simple ways to turn it around:

(Attend a support group meeting. It may be a meeting you thought was awful the last time you attended. Try it again, or try another meeting. Let yourself be surprised.

(Telephone a friend or a professional counselor who understands you and can offer immediate support and encouragement. Don't let false pride stop you from asking for this kind of help.

(Perform one task or duty that ought to be completed. If you're tired or deeply depressed, this

may take superhuman determination. It can also
break the logjam of procrastination.

(Help somebody. There must be something to this
kind of sharing because it launched the fellowship of
AA and still works whenever it's given a fair chance.

(Release any resentment or bitterness, no matter how
dear your grievances are to you. Ill will always
disguises and justifies itself in some manner, but we
can't conceal how sick it makes us.

(Read, pray, and act. Inspirational reading may set
your thinking straight, while doing something
positive and helpful will reinforce this new attitude.

7. Seven major human defects can serve as a checklist in
taking one's personal inventory. They are listed on page
48 of *Twelve Steps and Twelve Traditions*. Known as the
seven deadly sins, they are pride, greed, lust, anger,
gluttony, envy, and sloth.

It is surprising to find *sins* listed in an AA book, since
the fellowship has always taken the position that
alcoholism is a disease and that alcoholics are sick
people. But as Bill W. wrote in discussing these terms,
"All who are in the least reasonable will agree upon one
point: that there is plenty wrong with us alcoholics
about which plenty will have to be done if we are to
expect sobriety, progress, and any real ability to cope
with life." The purpose of using this list is merely to
categorize our principal defects, not to wallow in a bog
of condemnation while we repeatedly label ourselves as
sinners. One other important point: Most human

beings are guilty of these sins to some extent, so we are not calling ourselves unusually bad people when we accept this list of seven sins.

8. One way of simplifying service is to know that there are at least eight forms of it in AA:

   (talking during discussion meetings and one-on-one

   (listening to what others say and sensing their pain

   (speaking at lead meetings, the modern form of witnessing

   (writing in letters and journals

   (assisting, taking people to and from meetings

   (implementing, by running the meetings and taking care of coffee and other details

   (sharing personal details about our own lives

   (accepting completely any person who comes to the fellowship

9. Emotional immaturity has been targeted as a universal problem among alcoholics. It takes full commitment to the goal, but recovering alcoholics can grow in maturity. One can use nine simple questions to measure personal progress in this effort:

   (Am I controlling my anger more effectively, without resorting to violence, malicious acts, or destructive behavior?

  (Am I displaying more patience and an ability to work for long-term goals?

  (How is my perseverance? Am I sticking with things until I get them done?

  (Can I deal with unpleasantness, frustration, and even defeat?

  (Do I sense any growth in humility, perhaps saying "I was wrong" once in a while?

  (Am I able to make a decision now and live with it?

  (How reliable am I? Can I keep my promises? Do I have enough self-understanding not to make promises I cannot keep?

  (Can I accept the things I cannot change?

  (Have I found the courage to change the things that can and should be changed?

10. While there are millions of books in the world and thousands dealing with alcoholism, ten ought to be in every recovering alcoholic's possession, to be read and reviewed continuously:

  (*Alcoholics Anonymous,* AA's famous and virtually indispensable Big Book

  (*Twelve Steps and Twelve Traditions,* AA cofounder Bill W.'s discussion of how the program works

  (*As Bill Sees It,* further observations from Bill W.

❖ *Twenty-Four Hours a Day,* the meditation book that has been a reliable guide for more than forty years

❖ *Daily Reflections,* AA's new meditation book

❖ *The Sermon on the Mount,* by Emmet Fox, a book that the AA pioneers used for inspiration

❖ *Dr. Bob and the Good Oldtimers,* the biography of Dr. Bob Smith

❖ *'Pass It On,'* the biography of Bill W.

❖ *The Greatest Thing in the World,* by Henry Drummond, the inspirational book that Dr. Bob loved

❖ *As Man Thinketh,* by James Allen, a discussion of the profound effects of thought on the course of our lives

11. They're not easy to remember, but there are at least eleven statements of important truth in several places in *Alcoholics Anonymous,* the Big Book. Three appear on page 60 and are read at almost every meeting:

❖ "That we were alcoholic and could not manage our own lives."

❖ "That probably no human power could have relieved our alcoholism."

❖ "That God could and would if He were sought."

Two more appear in "Bill's Story" on page 12:

- "Why don't you choose your own conception of God?"

- "It was only a matter of being willing to believe in a Power greater than myself. Nothing more was required of me to make my beginning."

Each of these two statements reinforces the idea of God as we understand Him. These are further enhanced by four statements on page 47, in the chapter titled "We Agnostics":

- "When, therefore, we speak to you of God, we mean your own conception of God."

- "Do not let any prejudice you may have against spiritual terms deter you from honestly asking yourself what they mean to you."

- "At the start, this was all we needed to commence spiritual growth. . . ."

- "Afterward, we found ourselves accepting many things which then seemed entirely out of reach. That was growth, but if we wished to grow we had to begin somewhere."

Finally, on page 570, we'll find two important statements that deserve continuous repeating:

- "Willingness, honesty and open mindedness are the essentials of recovery. But these are indispensable."

This last statement, attributed to Herbert Spencer, is a warning to those whose intellectual pride can keep them from recovery:

("There is a principle which is a bar against all information, which is proof against all arguments and which cannot fail to keep a man in everlasting ignorance—that principle is contempt prior to investigation."

12. If there is a magic number in AA, it is twelve. There are the famous Twelve Steps, which are repeated at almost every AA meeting. There are also Twelve Traditions, not mentioned so often but always referred to for the guidance of the AA society. There are also Twelve Concepts of World Service, prepared by Bill W. later in life. There is increasing attention to the Twelve Promises, which are now read at many AA meetings. These promises were not even numbered when they were listed in the Big Book and it seems only coincidental that there are twelve of them. A fitting way to close this chapter on keeping it simple is to review these simple promises, which can be found on pages 83–84 of *Alcoholics Anonymous:*

> If we are painstaking about this phase of our development, we will be amazed before we are half way through. We are going to know a new freedom and a new happiness. We will not regret the past nor wish to shut the door on it. We will comprehend the word serenity and we will know peace. No matter how far down the scale we have gone, we will see how our

experience can benefit others. That feeling of uselessness and self-pity will disappear. We will lose interest in selfish things and gain interest in our fellows. Self-seeking will slip away. Our whole attitude and outlook upon life will change. Fear of people and of economic insecurity will leave us. We will intuitively know how to handle situations which used to baffle us. We will suddenly realize that God is doing for us what we could not do for ourselves.

Are these extravagant promises? We think not. They are being fulfilled among us—sometimes quickly, sometimes slowly. They will always materialize if we work for them.

Shouldn't It Be Easier Than This?

It's been hard for me to accept that recovery is about progress, not perfection. I've been in the program almost two years now and am still having my share of bad days. Hey, shouldn't it be easier than this?

I came into the program thinking if I stopped using, things would be 100 percent better. I still think that way sometimes—all or nothing, black or white, yes or no. I try to remember to quit looking for the magic. Today, my life is much simpler. My days of doubting whether recovery is worth it are fewer. Sobriety was just the first step; changing my life and how I deal with others and myself has been the hard part.

I have a job I like. I have real friends and I'm active in the program. This type of life agrees with me. But when I'm by myself too much, get into self-pity, and again think all or nothing, I get really stuck. They say "an addict alone is in bad company." When I'm like this I think, "What's the use?" I back myself into a corner of self-obsession and think there's no way out. I think I can't stand life's problems anymore, but then this program provides an answer and the bad times pass. I'm learning how to live with myself.

Before I came into the program I really had no freedom. I didn't understand the word. The only meaning it had for me was the idea of being released from prison or being able to fly. I like both those ideas, but the only things that gave me the illusion of freedom were alcohol and drugs. It never lasted because something always went bad when I was wasted. I was in prison, the prisoner of active addiction without knowing it.

I knew I was miserable, but I didn't know why. I thought I was under a curse and felt cut off from the rest of the human race. I was in a trap and desperate to get out. That meant I was at the mercy of other people's whims and knew how to be only what I thought other people wanted me to be. I was always being blown around by the winds of circumstance.

The very first experience with freedom in my life was when someone said to me, "Do you want to stop drinking and drugging?" and I said, "Yes," realizing that I really meant it. The second experience was when someone said to me, "You need never get wasted again." Both these ideas had never before reached my brain and it was the first glimpse of reality and sanity for a sick and desperate person.

The longer I stay in recovery, the more I learn about freedom. "Shouldn't it be easier than this?" is about freedom. The freedom to stay stuck, "awfulizing," or facing stinking thinking and bad times head on. Knowing is not enough; I must apply. Being willing is not enough; I must do.

When All Else Fails, Follow Directions

Why is recovery so difficult for some and seemingly easy for others? Like someone who uses a new recipe and wonders why the dish wasn't as good as the person's next door, the person may find that the directions are simple but fouled up easily if not followed.

One of the directions in the program is, "Don't get on the wagon, get on the program." The program directs you simply: First be honest with yourself, no more games, alibis, lies, or false promises! If you are honest with yourself, you can then turn your problems over to the Higher Power. This first direction is repeated over and over again, and yet many fail to follow the first direction.

The next direction is to lay out a program for addiction-free daily living. Next comes involving yourself in a program seeking to help others seeking recovery. It is said that ours is a simple program and the directions are easy to follow; but somehow too many try shortcuts, substitutions, and like the person with the new recipe, discover they substituted some ingredient or left out an important step. So again remember KISS: "Keep it simple, stupid." And when all else fails, follow directions.

K.I.S.S.

Keep it simple, stupid!

—Anonymous

When we were using, our addicted minds were too clever for their own good. They told us lies. They told us that we knew things we didn't, that we were strong when we weren't. The addicted mind tried to analyze recovery and find its fatal flaws. That way it could return to addiction with all the reasons why the program can't and shouldn't work. But the program doesn't have its foundation in this type of reasoning. Its foundation is faith, and faith defies reason. Reason is complicated. Faith is very simple.

Our addictions are clever, baffling, powerful, and very patient. Our program disciplines this addiction with the simple truth. We fight the addiction with honesty. Our program has revealed to us that truth is not complicated. It is simple. We should not dress the truth up in fancy clothes.

I want to keep it simple, just as it is. I won't use my clever mind to twist the truth. My program tells me that I need to keep it simple just as I found it.

Afterword

To some, seven slogans won't seem to be adequate instruments for navigating through the storm conditions that recovering people are likely to find in their lives. Many of these people will also be well-educated, sensitive persons who distrust simplistic answers and solutions.

Again, we must express the belief that the slogans are important because they embrace universal principles for good living. While the slogans are simple statements, the principles will find wide application and can become useful topics for endless discussions about life in recovery.

There is another point here that some of us found instructive. Often, when we felt turned off by simple slogans and methods of recovery, a little further self-examination showed that we were displaying a false intellectual pride to resist the program of recovery. Such false pride works for a time in a drinking or using environment, but it is quickly recognized and exposed among people who are truly recovering.

While the slogans and their underlying principles were a turnoff in our early days, they've usually turned out to play a major part in our growth and sobriety. Call them "shorthand for the Twelve Steps." Or accept S. I. Hayakawa's point that they're "shortcuts to a consensus." Whatever you call them, slogans have a role in human affairs as well as in Twelve Step programs. In looking at the thousands of slogans that people use, we even have to say that slogans are like a language unto themselves. The slogans have a special place in Twelve Step programs because they convey important principles that express our special truths. Far from sneering at the simplicity of slogans, we should be grateful that we have them as useful tools. Thanks to the people who coined or discovered these slogans and to the thousands who have passed them on, we don't have to search for these simple, useful guides ourselves. The work already has been done for us.

"The slogans work, if you let them." If you choose, that could also be a slogan to add to the seven we've presented here!

Other titles that may interest you . . .

Ebby
THE MAN WHO SPONSORED BILL W.
by Mel B.

This book uncovers the life of Ebby Thacher, focusing on his role in the development of the Alcoholics Anonymous fellowship. It includes the message of recovery Ebby Thacher gave to Bill W., cofounder of AA.

174 pages
Order no. 5699

Women Pioneers in Twelve Step Recovery
by Charlotte Hunter, Billye Jones, and Joan Zieger

This groundbreaking book is narrated by a number of women involved in the development of Twelve Step organizations such as Alcoholics Anonymous and Al-Anon.

208 pages
Order no. 5698

Harry Tiebout
THE COLLECTED WRITINGS

This book provides a fascinating glimpse into the writings of Harry Tiebout, a man whose ideas and insights shaped a pioneering contribution to recovery.

160 pages
Order no. 1119

For price and order information or a free catalog, please call our telephone representatives or visit our Web site at **www.hazelden.org**

◨ HAZELDEN®

1-800-328-9000   (Toll-Free U.S., Canada, and the Virgin Islands)

1-651-213-4000   (Outside the U.S. and Canada)

1-651-213-4590   (24-Hour Fax)

www.hazelden.org Visit our Web site and look for the Hazelden-Pittman Museum link where you will find an archive of materials that document the history of Hazelden, addiction in America, and the development of Alcoholics Anonymous.

15251 Pleasant Valley Road
P.O. Box 176
Center City, MN 55012-0176